Iota

93

Iota 93 2013:2

The Editorial Team

Nigel McLoughlin (Poetry Editor) is Professor of Creativity & Poetics at the University of Gloucestershire. He is the author of five poetry collections, the latest of which is *Chora: New & Selected Poems* (Templar, 2009). His work has been published in Ireland, UK, USA, Europe, Asia and Australia. He has guest edited for several journals including *The Black Mountain Review, The New Writer* and *Fortnight*.

Kate North (Reviews Editor) lectures in Creative Writing at Cardiff Metropolitan University. Her novel is *Eva Shell* (Cinnamon, 2008) and her poetry collection is *Bistro* (Cinnamon, 2012).

Angela France (Features Editor) is currently a PhD student and lecturer in Creative Writing at the University of Gloucestershire. She is a prize-winning poet who has published regularly in many of the leading journals in the UK and abroad. Her collections of poetry are, *Occupation* (Ragged Raven Press. 2009), *Lessons in Mallemaroking* (Nine Arches Press, 2011). and *Hide* (Nine Arches Press,2013).

Jane Weir (Fiction Editor) is an Anglo - Italian writer and freelance designer. Her poetry works include *The Way I Dressed During the Revolution (2005), Alice* (2006), *Before, Playing Romeo (2008)* and two poetic biographies *Walking the Block* (2008) and *Spine* (2012) based on the lives and creative work of Phyllis Barron and Dorothy Larcher, the modernist hand block printers.

Dan Sluman
is the current member of the Editorial Panel and a 26 year old poet based in Gloucestershire. His poems have appeared widely in journals, including *Cadaverine, Popshot, Shit Creek Review* and *Orbis*. His debut collection *Absence has a weight of its own*, was published through Nine Arches Press in 2012. He holds an MA from the University of Gloucestershire.

Alex McMillen is the publisher of Templar Poetry and Iota.

Contacting Iota

www.iotamagazine.co.uk
Editor: editor@iotamagazine.co.uk
Features: features@iotamagazine.co.uk
Reviews: reviews@iotamagazine.co.uk

Online Submissions Welcome
www.iotamagazine.co.uk/Submissions

Online Subscriptions Welcome
www.iotamagazine.co.uk/Subscriptions

Postal correspondence, Subscriptions and Submissions:
Iota Poetry
PO Box 7721
Matlock
DE4 9DD
Iota 93
www.iotamagazine.co.uk
www.templarpoetry.co.uk
ISBN 9781906285-66-1
ISSN 0266-2922 £6.99

Contents

Poetry

Interviews

Reviews

Editorial

Welcome to the new issue of *Iota*. In this edition we have gathered together work from twenty-six poets; twenty-eight if we include the featured poems from our interviewed poets Jo Bell and John Gallas. These poets range in experience from those who are just beginning to build a track record of publication to previous winners of the National Poetry Competition, and those with several collections to their credit. I'm glad to see several poets who have been previously published in Iotas past, return to these pages. There is a heady mix of styles and voices, and our reviews section again features discussions of some of the most interesting titles published over the last year or so.

Not long ago, Seamus Heaney passed away. On behalf of *Iota*, I'd like to extend our deepest sympathy to Marie, his wife, his children and his extended family. *Ar dheis Dé go raibh a anam uasal*. I can't claim to have known him, but like many others, I met him briefly on a couple of occasions, and found him a generous and charming man. He was down to earth, carried his education and his achievements lightly, and made time for others. It was difficult to grow up in Northern Ireland in the late 70s and 80s without encountering his work. 'Blackberry Picking', 'Death of a Naturalist' and 'Digging' were staple performance pieces which featured at *Feiseanna*. For the uninitiated, these are gatherings where children as young as seven or eight (I did once see an under 5 section) recite poems they have learned 'by heart' in open competition at that year's county '*Feis*'. Later, our generation found his poems on the 'O' Level and 'A' Level syllabi. He was an extremely important part of our induction into poetry, both as readers and as writers. There was really no way to avoid his influence. He is as close as it gets to a cultural icon for those of us who grew up in that time.

As the tributes accrued on facebook, in the press, and elsewhere, what struck me was that everyone had an anecdote to tell, and these, more often than not, showed the humanity of the man. He was very much a good skin, a *mensch*, one of 'us', or how we'd like to think of 'us'. It's not that the poetry was secondary or forgotten, that was talked about too, but somehow, people wanted to focus on him as a man, not just a celebrity, not just a Nobel laureate. There were obituaries too which foregrounded the achievements. the honours, the poetry; the fact that we had lost what many in the world saw as the greatest Irish poet since Yeats; but what caught my attention were the many personal and unofficial eulogies on the man from poets (and readers) around the internet, around the globe, which demonstrated the esteem in which he was held, not only for the work, but for his personal qualities. There were many stories of his modesty and generosity in his dealings with other poets and with those running events which were held up as a model for poets in their professional behaviour.

I must admit I added my own anecdote, which I recount again here by way of tribute: it comes from my observation of one small incident which illustrates the type of man he was. Not long after he won the Nobel Prize I remember standing outside a reading Heaney was due to give. As he arrived, flanked by what looked like 'minders' trying to whisk him away to the 'green room', a young boy stopped him for his autograph. He asked the boy his name and asked him what his favourite poem was and the boy replied "Mid-Term Break". "Mine too", Heaney said, "I'll read it later for you". The boy was absolutely beaming. And Heaney read the poem 'for his young friend' later. I'd be willing to bet that kid, wherever he is now, has an abiding memory of being made to feel important as a reader, and I'm sure, still carries an abiding love of Heaney's poetry.

Heaney leaves us with a body of work that revels in the music, energy and the feel of language. The work at once makes us feel anew our experiences of 'being in the world' and offers us a sense of the ineffable and the marvellous that might exist beyond our experience of it. By that I mean that when I read Heaney's poems, many of the ones I enjoy most offer a sense of the narrow spectrum along which human perception operates, and gives us a sense of that partial perception, and what we might be missing about the world, and about ourselves. His poems are imbued with the sense of honesty, decency and humanity that all those who encountered him found in the man who has left us; but he has left us with poems that will endure to delight those of us who are left, and those who will come hereafter.

Nigel McLoughlin

Poetry

Steve Sawyer's passion for poetry and the stage began at an early age. He has worked as an actor, stand-up comic and as a lecturer in philosophy and social science. His poems have been published in magazines including *Brittle Star, Iota, Long Poem* and *Tears in the Fence*. Steve's work reflects his strong ties with the north of England where he was born. He now lives in Sheffield.

Nostalgia for the Light

Sunglasses and bare shoulders,
rapid-fire dialect among the market stalls
on the day the Caravan of Death
came to Calama. A city and commune
of ancient pepper-trees and partridges,
the arched bone of a dancer's foot
and blueberries; wheat, fish and water
in the driest hot desert on earth.

ni pena ni miedo, written in the sand
with earthmoving equipment, in letters
so big they can only be read from the air
when threads of volcanic steam clear
and the desert opens its book of memory.

Goat bells, washing lines, motorbikes,
a caesarean section. A painter giving light
to a mouth in the plaza, on the day
a death squad did the bidding of a dictator
regaled by presidents, a prime minister
of Great Britain. *Neither shame nor fear*

inlaid in the desert, read by the stars.
The initial '*n*' with its sweeping downstroke,
windblown sand on the windward edge;
gentle angles, letters that glide and whorl,
working with the desert grain, looping out
of repose so each word remains unbroken.

Women of Calama, numb-blood pulsing,
driving as if in a blizzard, to hospitals,
wasteland and morgues: corridors, offices,
a basement of corpses. On the solitary road
into the desert, peyote visions of salt lakes,
seamless from the turquoise milk of the sky.
Baptismal snow on the observatory dome.

Astronomers tell us we live behind time;
search beyond the light for our source
in fragmentary stars, long dispersed.
In the Atacama's absolute desert, not a blade
of grass or weightless god. Not a gnat, bat
or bowling alley but the women of Calama
search below sand for a scintilla of bone,
with a hand-held plastic shovel. Husbands,
sons, brothers – a splinter of guitar finger –
the same calcium galaxies are made of;
pieces of unfinished laughter, a cheek bone
with the bullet lodged in, or something more:
the cellular memory of indigenous wars
lasting three centuries; pre-Columbian signs
of justice and renewal in the sudden light
of a tooth that becomes the entire universe.

If you trace the giant sweep and bend
of the text on the desert's open page –
five minutes to reach the *'i'*, at an easy pace –
run gently on the ineluctable soft berms,
three-, four-foot high to the next word,
heavy-bodied, giddy-headed,
you smell the white cap snowmelt, hear
the desert breathe lightly, the Milky Way
read softly. As for the poet?

I could say: Raul Zurita.

I could say: the dead that change places
with the living.

You would need to study dust.

Last Face I Will See

Steve Sawyer

In the eyes, I see green rice-stalks
and sunset-tender potatoes.
The lips are crossbows in the long grass,
the patience of endless rain. Face
of a warrior-queen or priest-king, who
would lean to the earth in a conical hat.
I hear the maddening agony
of brown water, leaping towards the sky
as hammocks quiver in tunnels of poetry
under enemy guns; the young girl who
saved the convoy by waving her torch,
bringing down the bombs on herself.

In the eyes, I see green rice-stalks
and sunset-tender potatoes. A helmet
floats in the river dark, cast by the tip
of the nose, where children play Dragons
and Snakes and the string of the dan bau
glides. I fear this giant face I love:
a furrowed oceanic island, hiding
a thousand lightning bolts. Helicopters
flying around the nose, mosquitoes
seeking warm human-strains, the call –
answer refrains of ancient communal songs,
words cracking in the banana groves,
pagoda bells and endless shapes,
hues of green and waves of blue.
The vertical-striped cheeks are rice fields
where cows eat grass from graves,
and ancestral souls take a shortcut
to the far side of the Monkey-bridge,
that old stretch of road, houses on stilts,
a glimpse of knitting, torn posters
describing the life of the Buddha, adorning
the walls; the crossing-pass straight ahead.

In the eyes, I see green rice-stalks
and sunset-tender potatoes. A wristwatch,
and canvas shoe in a ration box. The scent
of grapefruit blossoms rising-in-circles,

at that turn in the road where the young girl
waved her torch. The leopard silence
of this peasant fighter; that old stretch
of road. It would take a tenth of a second
for the eyelids to move a millimetre – close.

Central Lending

Steve Sawyer

Yesterday morning I am at the keys
in main Lending when I hear the ripped vowel
of a seagull's cry over calm water.

I look around the table, see a young woman
the colour of rosewood, tears of barley pearl,
her cheeks diffusing the light of hot flesh.

Users of the computer suite are staring at her
and one another, as if she were flailing her limbs
like ocean-rich kelp or conjuring a marmoset
from her tunic sleeve. Keyboards of the People's
Network, clack. A hole-punch bolts a perfect 'O'.
Spectacles ride smiles and a bracelet leaps
on a wrist by the One-Week-Loan Best-Sellers.

A sharp intake of breath breaks into sobbing –
like the last half-dozen strokes of a saw blade
ascending the scale before it draws on air.
Strangely, I anticipate it; need it more
than I needed a Patagonian llama to shamble
through this library door *en route* for Music and Film.

The people round the table stare at me now
as well as her, as if she and I were one.
Vowels drift like dandelion seeds to fade
between Poetry and Adventure. I go to her:
scalded eyes like mineral springs, disbelieving,
the hot liquid sluicing through her eye lashes;
the crackle of leather around a shoulder,
under an arm, as someone reaches for a key.

I return to my seat, nodding assuredly
like a dashboard dog. Ker-ching! A fine paid.
Clunk! A date stamped. A lion is killing a gazelle
on the monitor to my left; the girl's arms waving
at counter-staff, tears like melting rouge
on her face; her SOS turning to jubilation:
*It's ok, I've done it – it's ok! Thank you
so much.* Laughter round the table, a tower
of birds in a basement of books.

I want to give her my apple fritter, to celebrate
these moments that contain her happiness
and what the day will bring –
but I am dancing with the tigress in the sun.

The Wedding Song of Whirlow Park.

Steve Sawyer

Dad, come on, dad, come on, mum – run.
What a shock to realise that I was this 'dad'
– a woman calling, waving – on the lawn
facing the oblong forecourt at the front
of the estate, where I'd been sitting
on a park-bench, dedicated to the memory
of A Giant of a Dog, as the chrome grilles
and cream tail-fins of the stretch-limousines
oozed-up the gravel drive like hammerhead sharks.
Then, from the side of the house, the men
in frockcoats, swallows drinking in flight;
women, hand-signing for a draw
on a shared cigarette: low v-line necks
and butterscotch calves, dresses of gold
and lavender, sleeveless and purple, ruby
and strapless. One: ivory, mermaid tight,
thighs of nude pink in the sunshine.

It must have been the timbre of her voice:
Dad – come on! Such a tender imperative
that lit that sense that I was 'him' – this 'dad',
who's standing next to me - and that 'we'
were 'they', this whirlpool of tree ferns
and caspia, pink candles and lumps of butter,
soft, wide-brimmed black hats at 26 degrees.
Why don't they just ask me to leave?
I'm not one of them; I'm older and younger,
louder when vulgar; mostly, say nothing
at all. Photographs! Caught, writing my
escape, a dog bowl of stagnant water
at my feet. The serrated skyline
of marching pines with associating blues,
greens and variegated shading, bordering
the lawns. Ponds that teem with water fowl,
reflect yellow fleeces of laburnum that break up,
come together. I feel I know these guests
I haven't met: iron-bridge direct, vowels
hammer-bounced flat for a tang; that roar
of the earth, let-me-begin-again laughter.

I stare into the baize-green, mid-distance:
the little helpers, holding the bridal train above
rolling lawns; the married couple, ascending
flights of steps, thumbs-up to applause;
one woman – I return to this one woman –
cropped, dark hair; a pink-mauve gown,
with halterneck. A pulse of sadness in her
chanting eyes. Her smoker's husky laughter,
scratched and dry, buffed up to a fine sheen
on a roll, mellowing out at the tail end
like a sea-bell wrapped in harbour mist.
Her mouth disappears in sunshine.
Words bluster, whisper; a kissed cheek,
a top hat, then she's smaller, diminished
by distance, in a space between daylight's
bare-shoulders. I imagine all the people
she has known: What was his name?
Where did they go? How close you can get
to see-through pink ears, still feel alone
and related. She will see them again
in Spanish cathedrals, night train-windows.

Dad, come on, dad, come on, mum – run.
We fill the spaces between lilies
and thumbs, Canada Geese that are not
to be touched and two wooden bears
for the children. Leave behind eyes that pour
through wild roses and bright green hearts
on the water: *Tell us when. Just smile.*
Radio news in the tea room: what the bride
is wearing at that other wedding, further
than the far side of the soul. I climb out
of myself, pick my way between gloves
of white lightening, envelopes, marmalade,
a baby crawling on the grass.

This elderly man in a plush weave of cloth
that breathes for him; no sense of concern
at sitting far removed from his children
and their children; staring at the azure sky,

sensing the moment reaching back
to contain these lives, forward
to evening laughter, a river of words
without language, that softens as he walks
in freckled light among the pines.

The Iron Woman

Steve Sawyer

Waiting for the phone to ring in the Miner's Welfare –
the men told, last moment, of the night's mass-picket:
grabbing coats, thrown about on cratered roads, hands
pressed against the roof, as we swerved past haulage yards,
treatment plants, the anthracite air leaking darkness

into ineffable fathoms. Picket of pale smiles, voices
of fiery clouds, the blood in my head cooling, crosswinds
asking if something will happen. I was with Police Watch
organised to observe the policing of pickets, the coppers
were in Transits, eyes triggered, fishing-out bits of sandwich

from between their teeth. I saw her cycle towards us
in the early hours, to picket the night shift going in.
Her silhouette softening under fence lights – Women
Against Pit Closures, clapping – to dismount at the gates,
embrace her comrades on the line, time backed into a corner.

She must have been in her eighties. Front row, third left.
Same seat, row, teacher, slate; a spire she can no longer see.
Orchestras, chapel choirs, dance nights at the Greystones.
Her husband's lungs ripping themselves inside-out
on summer nights. Elvis in the Closed Shop taproom: she

danced to Blue Suede Shoes. She's as live to me as the guilt
I feel for trying to escape – not the people – the mining life,
through the promise-lie of education, to stumble upon myself
in a stranger on Collegiate Crescent, speaking a language
that wasn't my own, nor was it his. She carries me home:

coal and a chicken in our handlebar basket. I carry her
in coffee spoons, sleeplessness, a love of nocturnal beasts
that run against the odds. I see her in the childhood of stars,
a spinal canal of grassed-over spoils, words I mine.
Cycling past the pithead baths the miners built themselves,

gutted by vandals; a sculpted half-wheel – Red Road radio:
music like it used to be; a car swerves, beeps its horn,
an old willow uprooted by the storm; pumping her legs –
riding like dancing; the listed Victorian colliery offices
and clock tower, her silken feet light on her hips and heart.

Christopher James was born in Paisley in 1975. Educated at Newcastle and UEA, he won the National Poetry Competition in 2008, the Bridport Prize (2002) and the Ledbury prize twice. His books include *Farewell to the Earth* (Arc, 2011) and *England Underwater* (Templar, 2012). He was the recipient of an Eric Gregory Award in 2002.

The Nurse Who Sold The Atlantic Ocean

She places a small ad in *The Lady*:
'For sale: one ocean, several careless owners.
Would suit woman of limited means
but extravagant taste. Will negotiate.'
A week later, she's on a train west,
sipping Earl Grey from the cap of a flask.
She peers up at the mackerel sky.

In her bag, she has packed bandages,
swabs, a sharps box in case of mishap.
At the station she's met by a swimmer
with long grey hair and of magnificent build.
Her eyes are as soft as the last glimpse of sun
above the hills. They sit a long time on
the Atlantic's crumpled yellow shore.

The nurse accepts her payment: white wine,
bream, a small painting of boats out to sea.
The swimmer confesses: 'I've trespassed
too long in its cold grey folds.' Going back
the nurse clicks opens her case, draws out
a vial of water, flicks it once and holds
what's left of her ocean swarming at the moon.

Surfing The Bore

Christopher James

Buoyed on the moon-tide,
Gloucestershire passed
in a dreaming:

the drowning willows waved us on.
Past Purton and Etloe,
we took the bend at Blaize-Bailey

like geese landing on water
while the Bore swamped the banks,
and scattered the cows.

Poised on the lip of the Severn,
we were Neptune's men, pulled
by dolphins on threads of gold.

Like fishing flies cast upstream
we rode the river, the wave
skirmishing at our heels.

And through the spray we glimpsed
the ghost of Jack Churchill,
the first to tame the Bore,

sword drawn, one arm raised,
leading the charge like Cardigan
at the head of the Light Brigade.

Abegail Morley's first collection, *How to Pour Madness into a Teacup* (Cinnamon) was shortlisted for the Forward Prize Best First Collection; her second *Snow Child* (2011) is published by Pindrop Press. *Eva and George: Sketches in Pen and Brush* (Pindrop, 2013) is an ekphrastic collection based on the work of George Grosz.

Summer

The corn scrapes our shins.
We've no reason to go back.
Now you're here, we spend the summer
in the fields, far from our houses
where no-one can see.

We rub mud on naked arms;
put stripes across our faces
blood red clay over our noses,
pull back our hair.

We march by the river, sun scalds
our scalps and necks. From the back
I can tell you're not a boy;
your legs are too skinny and your
hips widening gently.

You thrash the corn with a slender
branch of willow - air whips round your head
faster, faster, you love the noise.
Sap spills in your palm.

We thrust our feet in the water,
kick until we're soaked. Next thing
you're on the bridge, toes over its edge
holding yourself still against the breeze.

You bend slightly, unlock your knees, leap.
You drop slowly through the air
almost as if it's trying to catch you.

Explanation

Abegail Morley

My body hasn't learnt his, doesn't know
where he can take it. So the fall, as he calls it,
shears skin from bone and bone from body, leaves me glazed –

a fish gupping water, stunned by the sweep of tide that turns
without looking at its own reflection - dragging me with it.
So I wait for time's throat to tell me it's through,

for his mouth to say it no longer wants mine,
no longer craves me. It's easy for me to split this wave,
slip through the sea's thin lining. If it's not this wave,

then the next or the next or the next.

The Love Child

Abegail Morley

I store the potato, peeled, cut from itself, wrapped in polythene.
When I open the fridge the motion of the door rocks it
back and forth like a skull. Tonight on my way home
I nod to the grocer who, drenched in the electric light,

sprouts wings like Phanes. His hands are grubby, old
and I wonder how they'd feel on my body, what he'd say
about the empty fruit bowl, how he'd bend to kiss
the top of my head while checking my kitchen:

a Cafetiere, wine, bread. I know in the morning
those fingers will plunge down the coffee
and I'll smell it here at the top of the house and hope
he doesn't take milk and I'll pray he doesn't open the fridge.

But I know he'll fan out his fat hands, hold the hollows
of the fontanelles, cradle it like a baby's head.

Abegail Morley

Here is a slice of mouse hippocampus

In the German Hygiene Museum
they're displaying a Brainbow –
floodlighting bodies from the inside
out. They've slices of brain

in Tupperware boxes in freezers
in basements and librarians
are cataloguing stem cells
according to size and colour.

On a large screen an epileptic woman
is lit up like a firework – an explosion
of neurons bursting across the room.
This is the anatomy of light.

**Brainbow technique colours individual neurons*

Chris Rice was a founder member of the Pembridge Poetry group in the mid 1970s with Robert Greacen and Matthew Sweeney. He has had poems in many magazines and journals, most recently *The London Magazine*, *Acumen* and *Smiths Knoll*. In 2011, he was joint-winner of the Friends of Richmond Park 50th Anniversary Poetry Prize.

Decoy

Every night I see them
at my window, looking in,
expecting invitations, raincoat
collars slapping at their faces
in the wind. Why not draw
the curtains on them, pull
my headphones on, move my chair
to corners their accusing gaze
can't reach? I'd burn the wind
that buffets them to ashes
if I could, but leave this chair
half-turned, half-facing noses
pressed like snails against the glass?
I wish they'd understand
that, even though I have the key,
the door is not within my power
to open. I have to sit here, object
of chill gazes I cannot return,
because they know, as I do not,
I've always been a decoy
set to draw attention from myself,
helplessly observed by those
who live in my imagination
wanting me to think I live in theirs.

Nomad

I bask in orange sunlight
on a bridge of white enamel,
watch the northbound passages
of ships that seem to glide
across the land. Everything
is still – a little eerie. Shadows
sprout like black and violet
flowers in the sand. Two men
in the distance leave a rusty
iron construction, head my way,
their shadows long black bony
fingers aimed at me. A small lake
choked with reeds behind me
rids itself of fishing boats. A boy
strains to retrieve a sinking oar.
A man sits cross-legged in the bow,
coiling twine around a broken net.

I'm shrinking fast.
I span horizons on all sides.
I'm in the middle of a vast arena
yet feel somehow at its rim,
peering over railings at a sandpit
in whose centre I'm a dot.
The land belongs to scorpions
and those who walk barefoot
among them. Nothing here
belongs to me, which is why
I call it home, finding beauty
in the spray that others going
somewhere leave behind.

Waxwing

You *look* filled with fruit, flushed and swollen
like an uncle after Christmas dinner,
musketballs of orange berries rolling down your throat,
and yet you are a dandy little fellow with your panto-
villain make-up, your feathers splashed
with sauce and pudding dipped in cold champagne.

People, slanting, mackintoshed and hooded, hurry
by. One or two perhaps toss muttered glances,
I don't know. I'm busy being mesmerised
by miracles unfolding overhead. Waxwings
– six or seven of them – swoop head-high
between the buses on the London Road, bugling

for stragglers like you. One last chandelier of fruit,
you spring as from a catapult, rise, as if controlled
by wires, between vanilla towers of brick
and, wings a-blur and wobbling, as if about to
jettison the fat pink luggage of yourself, fly
until you're nothing but a dimple in the London sky

that ripples with the muffled thump of pulses
driving you like moths not to a lantern
but a sea that lies in ambush, waiting for its feast
of fruit to drop exhausted to the iced saliva
of its lips, stripping sky of you
as you once stripped our trees of berries …

Jeffrey Alfier has work appearing or forthcoming in *Poetry Ireland Review*, *Connecticut Review*, and *South Carolina Review*. His latest chapbook is *The City Without Her* (Kindred Spirit Press, 2012), and his first full-length book of poems, *The Wolf Yearling*, is forthcoming from Pecan Grove Press.

Susquehanna River Town

Ours are ordinary streets of sparrow nests
and steeples, the hunger of all-night cafés,
half-mast flags that gave up on the wind
today, men in default of deeds of trust,
and bridge piers that have forgotten the river.

Farmers shoulder pallets of strawberries
past a Victorian hotel. They hope
for buyers among the thin foot traffic,
announcing their crop in gusted shouts
as curtains flutter from open windows.

And here I am, blessed to simply carry on,
sunlight coursing over me like grace as I stride
through an updraft of leaves that shamble
the hotel doorway, glancing up, deluded
into believing a woman above me is waving.

The Soldier Willie McCausland Speaks of the Dancer He Can't Take Home

Watching you twist inverted
toward the stage floor, my eyes
swear pole dancing comes
down to the physics of friction.

Baby, when you go on smoke
break inside that fenced
courtyard out back, I get lonely
as a pin pulled from a grenade.

As you reemerge inside, late
sunlight slips you through
a chorus of shadows. You pace
in a slow mercy toward my chair.

I lower the Drambuie from my lips
to let your breath blur with mine.
You, owner of pliant monikers,
how often you have saved men

from what they go home to, well before
you quit some a.m. hour, exit under
a bouncer's eye, your skin's glow dim,
the last light to go out in a ghost town.

Death Valley Interlude: The Panamint Range

Into bonedust air, bright as spun glass,
I began my climb beyond Badwater Spring,
my relief map a broken web of elevations.
Nonhuman tracks over dunes of Mesquite Flat
could warn wanderers even ghosts die of thirst.

The cab of a '61 Dodge is a carapace of rust
shipwrecked in the sun. Desert holly walks
its silver shards of leaves up a dark lava slope.
Wind that slips crossbeams of shuttered gypsum
mines tastes of ancient salt and rainspouts.

Sun drops behind my last switchback
of the day. Constellations transpire one star
at a time, as if surfacing from the sea.
In a cold wind my campfire glows against
foraged carrion in the teeth of a kit fox.

Its eyes follow my hands into the light.

Making West Side Industrial, Last Afternoon of Summer

The newest hire at a Mopar supply, I'm headed
uptown, Jefferson Avenue, waiting at Delray
crossing on my Indian motorbike – rebuilt
like everything else – for a CSX train to lumber
past. I seem to ride not pavement, but the very
breath of this August heat wave that herds
crowds to Belle Isle, no relief off the river,
or its other banks, Canada never flagging
like we do, the mercury unfazed, autumn
just a rumor summer's thrown off like a chump.

My uncle swears we're all here to redeem
what we can, but he quit this city, its brick-
walled highways I take to work, side streets
where crime comes heavy with hunger.
Down the road now, last stoplight before my shift,
I'll watch a woman's blue heels strike crosswalk
yellow, sparking colors over Trumbull Street gray.
I rev my engine, but she's immured, as if hastened
steps alone could to lift her from the city,
or all the eyes that blink and look back.

Jennie Owen is a University Lecturer in Creative Writing, and has been a Senior Editor for *Black Market Review* since 2008. She lives in Mawdesley, Lancashire and is a member of Skelmersdale Writers.

The Tiger in the Lounge

Come to tea? No not this one.
This threat has been here all along, all
copper flash-fire eyes, sleeking
behind the sofa. When he licks his fur
with a tongue as rough as pine cones,
his rusty breath scours. He eyes the baby,
rolling it in his bumble bee tail.
Gentle now, he arches his back,
so as not to unsettle tea cups,
set saucers rattling. But,
when roused, Rousseau could not
do him justice. A pad, half-moon
dagger-clawed, the size of a dinner plate,
groans the table to submission.
His grisly smile of teeth and blood.

Subterranean Dreams

We meet at the cusp, flinching at the rain
An orange night rat, King of tunnels, one
of a dozen knotted tails. Face a smut
scutting the points and the joints, greasing
silver and black luges. Joyful in your coal,
now you squint and shiver in a thready dawn.
Bagged up lint and human silks, last nights
burger underfoot. The market clang clangs.

Waiting inside, Damien's dream of living art
behind Perspex, a formaldehyde day walker.
The blue nylon mullah fillets paperwork,
corners flick snicker flick. As blind as the rest
hooking ducks behind his eyes, with the boy
miles away. Weekend thoughts nourish us, as
minutes tap, fleeing under carrion fingers.

We are your phantoms, descending into the
coral ping, shuttle rattle. Hurdles alert, chics,
tokens swooshed. Doze, cow upright, eyes
narrowed at billboard caterpillars. A collective
clench of suits shot through with ties. No
mouth above the neck, bristle coppice stop. Stop.
Expelled, repelled, shot-loaded out. A foam of
whining human jetsam, shimmers and steams.

Roger Elkin has won 45 First Prizes and several awards internationally, including the *Sylvia Plath Award for Poems about Women*, and the *Howard Sergeant Memorial Award for Services to Poetry* (1987). His collections include Fixing Things (2012); Marking Time (2012); and Bird in the Hand (2012). Editor of *Envoi*, (1991-2006), he is available for readings, workshops and poetry competition adjudication.

from ... Taxonomy of Famine Diseases

"The total of those who died ... of famine diseases will never be known, but probably about ten times more died of disease than of starvation."

C. Woodham-Smith, ***The Great Hunger****, (1962), page 204*

I *Scurvy*

cos dhub in Gaelic: black leg,
after the dark markings – crimson through to sloe –
of burst blood vessels blotching leg lengths
as high as mid-thigh, with great pain from inflamed joints.

Sometimes *purpura,* from Latin for purple:
observed in spongy gums (touched – even gently – they bleed)
between mouth lesions, and contrasting angrily
with those whitish islands of ulcers
on gums, throat and tongue;

and in splotches of purpuric eruption – stinging, livid, sore -
on hands, face and chest.

Either way, bleeding from backsides:
haw-red, scarlet, carmine.

Colourful stuff, this.

II *Bacillary Dysentery*

More colour:

the bloody flux: in Gaelic, *ruith fola*
sourced by bad food, and excrement traces on hands
and from faeces of flies;

diagnosed by galaxies on cabin floors
of blood-splats hardening from damson to scabby black;

but mostly invisible, hidden inside intestinal walls
where became inflamed in ulcerated honeycombs;

and witnessed, outwardly, by gradual marasmus
and the pain on faces while scowling
from bowel colic and rising drifts of gripe

till visible: the "looseness" –
liquid-thin mucus the rinsed-in-water colour of raw meat:
clear evidence internal gangrene had set in:

then shitting selves to non-existence.

Eric Paul Shaffer is author of *Lahaina Noon* (2005) and *Portable Planet* (2000). His poems appear in *Slate, North American Review, Ploughshares, Poetry East, Rattle, The Sun Magazine*, and more than twenty reviews in Australia, Canada, England, Ireland, Japan, New Zealand, Scotland, and Wales. He teaches at Honolulu Community College.

A Silver Flask

Of the dead, there is hardly more to say. The man was our appointed poet,
and our hallowed piles of buttressed stone ring hollow
as we stroll the halls he staggered. Each narrow oaken office door names
one more lettered, learned man schooled in definitions of "fool,"
"irony," and "comedy," and all taught the gist of our poet, our campus clown,

our dumpy ass in the soiled brown slacks of scuttlebutt. Dead drunks reek,
yet we indulge their sentimental tales. We linger fondly on stairs
ours bloodied once in a tumble of robes and sashes and stone-cracked skull.
None can tell how much plaid he peeked beneath or how many shots

he stole from freezers stocked with vodka, though his lines lifted skirts
and eyebrows less often than his drinking did. He dressed
our spectacles and brought rude, boozy measure to the depth and breadth
of our successes. We marked his steady wake of brittle books,
smirked at his famed, forgivable contempt for classrooms filled with poets

who read no verse, and ignored the volumes he loved and lent and lost,
yet we whispered of the crisp winter morning he wept in class
at forlorn lines of some scribbler long, long dead. He was
the added dash to our committees and catalogs, to our storied, shaded lanes.

Beneath pediments scaled with ancient words, he lurched and leaned.
His, the snore through windy speeches we endured. His, the stumbling step,
the fumble of a treasured tea cup, the vomit in the salad forks,
and rich red carpet swept with elbows, knees, and shirt-tails in a slow,
sodden crawl beneath the banquet board. Among our ivy and elms,

the man was our monument to the chaos we critique, and his death
is prelude to our own proud pageants, yet he was our poet.
He lived the life we urged him to live. His torments are our footnotes,
his laments, our literature, and our only secret is the gift of a silver flask.

The Dark Side Isn't Always

for Karen Joy Fowler

The dark side isn't always
dark, for the moon rotates exactly once
with every revolution around the planet.

When the face we see is full of light,
stars pale near the moon.

When the face is dark, the moon is new
and darkness visible, yet mystery remains
plain in the phases of shadow and sun

on the face hidden by the faces we see.
As we see only one face of the moon,
the unknown gazes always away

from sky-cast glances to confirm bearings
on Earth. Seeing what we think we see,
we see only half of what's there.

When the moon is new, skies blacken
with stars, and fire flares on the dark side

no one knows the sun illuminates,
one far face none see from here –
a dark moon now, a full moon new.

Rosamund Brown completed an MA in Creative Writing in 2010, producing a final poetry collection about the county of Shropshire. This led to her becoming a founder member of the Shrewsbury Museum Writers' Group and her work being featured in a 2012 exhibition, 'Impressions'. She has been published in several magazines.

Crosby Beach

After Antony Gormley

oh you
forgotten soldiers
waiting and watching
the horizon not blinking
when tugs tug ships chocked with containers
yes you maintain your gaze while suffering abuse
a scarf on one a condom on another and the lunar torture
waves against faces again and again upright coma victims
your nightmare repeats now now now shell-shocked soaked
but still hopeful the water blocks voices that might wake
you so you drown slipping off your pedestals to sink
into the muddy sand where worms will mark
your end scribbling with their casts
he was here please keep waiting
and watching always naked
your rust is beautiful
beautiful

Hair

Missionary,
I twist your boyish nape-curls
with my fingers,
secretly making a ring around the fourth.

Your mother says you're thinning on top;
ageing, she calls it.
I call it a big tick
in the virility box.

Besides,
I mainly care
for your facial hair.
Try not to shave,
for I swear that nestled in your beautiful red beard
are all our future children.
Keep them warm for me.

Ben Simmons is from Donegal and a master graduate from the National University of Ireland Galway. He began writing in his early teens in a local writers group. Ben received his first publication in Salmon *Poetry's Dogs Singing: A Tribute Anthology* (2010) and continues to write poetry, fiction and drama.

Infant-esse

White tipped wings lap against me,
gulls cry 'mother' from my lips,
a trailing skirt held below the knee,
dips into the cold steel water
from the slope of the shore to the sea

A left hand red and ready, grips
some unknown life she had before me
smoothed by water, sand forgets her
steps through shores of drifting memory,
the tide reverberates against the quay

I am chased into it by the ships
balanced on the curve of the earth.

The Night

Ben Simmons

The burly day is a man who,
in his hands, condenses all mystery
into a ball no larger that his head.
He grips the dark hours on either side;
he stares and he wonders
at all the shadowed forms,
plucking them out one by one
through the sunrise and twilight,
of his marble eyes.

Eluned Rees taught drama, before moving to Wales and becoming a dry stone waller in the Brecon Beacons. She completed an MA in Creative Writing at Bath Spa University and has had a number of poems published. She is currently writing a novel.

Children are Transgenic

Arms, wings raised
like spinnakers,
children quarter the compass
like proud old warships
unable to dissemble –
lifting and dipping
their keels
with the swell.

Pitched-up on shingle
at Southsea beach
they jerk like fish
hitting the deck –
they're crossed
with all sorts: flyers,
swimmers, creepers –
slow to graft
the human limb.

They smell over-sweet
like old juice
on the breath
of cider drinkers
mouthing endearments.

It's the sunset protocol:
someone must fire
the salute –
whistle-up an obedient
moon. Children
can't be counted on –
not waiting to be lit,
they shoot-up like shamans
or distress flares
over an un-winking sea.

St. David's Head

Eluned Rees

I

On the last slab of flat earth
the cathedral welcomes all
of the soon-to-fall.

Congregations tumble out
into the stink of wild garlic –
head for cliffs where copper rock
collapses into the westerly void.

They stare down at seals
which swivel and dive,
overflowing into the surf –
bellies up, gazing back
at the gazers, telling them:

This will never be your game.

II

Worshippers climb
down steps chiselled
out of the over-hang,
arch their backs
to the sun like lazy,
soft-spined cats
forgetting their terror
of tidal waters.

Collared to rock,
the Porth Justinian lifeboat
is bunched-up;
a mastiff poised
above black waves
to vault over names
embedded in rock –
those lost, those saved.

Graham Burchell was born in Canterbury and now lives in Dawlish, Devon. He has an M.A. in Creative Writing from Bath Spa University. His latest collection *The Chongololo Club* was published by Pindrop Press in June 2012. He is the 2012/13 Canterbury Festival Poet of the Year.

Night Ride To Teignmouth With Keats

On top of the coach, wedged between the fabrics
of others and packages in wicker, leather and wood,
there is room only for breath, rain and the wind
that draws discomfort like a purse string.

I touch his arm, smell the damp in his greatcoat
through my fingertips. He'll never know. I am ghost.
I've clawed back time to see his skin in the night -
smooth and cold - stones in a streambed.

I hear the harsh compression of his lungs,
sense melancholy behind eyes that flicker.
His and all the other heads are bowed.
Those seats could be pews in a roofless church.

Inside, in the dry, a corpulent man smokes, reeks
of powder and porter. He rubs against a woman
clutching a bible that she'll not open,
even when the white sky of morning comes.

Opposite, a Wesleyan priest with a fixed scowl,
journeys with a younger man whose nose needs dabbing,
who may be a relative. They do not converse
but sometimes growl, like coach wheels riding stones.

All complain when those same wheels drop into ruts.
A wife across from the poet, sleepy in the rain,
tightens the grip on her child. Her husband
digs deeper into the scruff of a fresh dead hare.

To End The Year

Lights on at midday
minor key music of dripping water outside
leafless gloom and me thinking of an ark
and its inner stink of wet fur

of fields as full-soaked sponges
of how it would be to live in a brook-side cottage
with flood red as potter's slip
that defies a closed door

that rudely checks out a snug front room
before pushing onwards into the kitchen
of how it would be to live outside
day and night like a bird or a slug

when the rain abates a bit
I'll go down the town to see
hope the brook has burst its banks
put on a show   a red silt party

I find it feisty as expected
Riding the rim like a bath about to overflow
it has a new shape there are hummocks
of brown dash and eddies never there before

it scuffs the underside of an iron bridge
hurries like molten chocolate
over the low falls
spills at the edges

a bright red ball bobs defiant
refuses to join twigs wood waste
an entire leafless shrub like a hill-giant's beard
on that journey to the sea

black swans geese and ducks sit
either side on the lawn on the banks
spectators wondering
in their bird-brain way of things

on my return there is not one red ball bobbing
two in orange have joined
I realise they are bulbs sucked
from a string of cross-banding coloured lights

they're an unexpected trinity
bright play in the mid-winter
God chose the colours

Joseph Minden lives and works in Cambridge.
These are his first published poems.

Remission

I came again and found the lake unfrozen
but not seen completely – just partly
visible through a gap in the trees,

that the agitation of the water's surface
made clear the constancy of the light:
the water moved, you felt the light held still.

What I saw was what was in interstices
between the leaves assembling
like pairs of hands trying to make frames.

In one point, the ripples seemed
to take the water down into a shadow
kept in its own surface, making cellar

steps and three seedy neon arrows
out of bands pushing against the light.
The world, as it was here, leant

out of itself, the lake gathered into
folds of taffeta and passed the movement
of the wish to be at rest into the land.

Preface

Joseph Minden

It is what we were made for, every sense
appointed to assess the works of nature,
weigh and measure, parcel into memory
its parts, for parsing when required by reason,
keen in turn to blunt the edge of error,
to face concealed methods as a glass.

But take, for instance, sight. It needs the glass
I bring to focus to augment it. Sense,
declined from primal accuracy through error
and the innate corruption of our nature,
failing, peddles falsehoods on to reason
and falsely stocks the aisles of memory.

The same decay has not spared memory –
which either cannot hold retained, like glass,
its images, or offers up to reason
travesties of records made by sense –
nor reason, whose own limits faced with nature
circumscribe what we unlock from error.

Solid definitions reek of error,
the alchemical credulity of memory,
far removed from evidence's nature:
I haul up from the well-shaft of this glass
my first attempts to amplify our sense
and build on sense conclusions fit for reason,

to render apprehensible to reason
its own world's design free from error,
to radically refine with art the sense
which hands material to memory,
and clear to the transparency of glass
reason's troubled interface with nature.

I mean to make a start: that is the nature
and the hope of this small work, the reason
I have cared to study through the glass,
though all endeavour bears the mysteries of error,
terra incognita, memory,
at root the prodigality of sense.

Nature keeps itself beyond our error.
I steel my reason for the lair of memory
and set against the glass a wanting sense.

Wild Oat

I am the one who watches where no eyes watch.
The sky rolls over me, making
and unmaking maps. It does not feel the scratch
at its foot. I have fractured out of nothing
and lace it with myself. When the wind
grows absent-minded, I am the trace
it leaves, a fleck of form suspended in space.

I know about substance hidden in air, the fork
of a swallow's tail, nicked out of absence like smoke
cut from smoke. I've shafted down my stalk
against the breeze, opened my hollow throat
and hung out these thin arms with a roost
of leaves to prove this sudden journeywork,
this claiming of direction from the dark.

I was itinerant and loose. I came
from carried water – look at how I hang
bearing its changing weight, the dry and the damp.
Now, on each side is the husk of a wing.
Taking shape, I sought to speak the language
of shapes, to hold rooted and precise
all formless possibilities of flight.

Holly Corfield Carr was born in Stafford in 1987. She received an Eric Gregory Award from the Society of Authors in 2012 and is currently working in collaboration with visual artists and creative technologists as writer-in-residence at Spike Island, supported by Arts Council England.

Antilabe

A raw gauze   pinned at four corners;
    this wet tarpaulin splits   as we slip
the blade of a toe   through its skin.

We lower ourselves   into scalloped space;
    palms till at the surface,   cupping cold light,
the crush of   breath.

A man with bristling epaulettes   breaststrokes
    standing upright,   drawing worn circles
with heavy arms, separating sons,   long grown.

A second man slowly windmills   between us,
    lifting an arm   in languorous backstroke,
half halts   halfway

with his hand angled   heavily, offering
    a loose spray   of fingers
and waits for the kiss.

I watch you swim   from the deep end;
    a neat crest   bowls before you
like jelly,   slack with heat in the pan.

Brow down,   your face is hidden
    amongst the shapes   breath takes
under the slap and sluice   of the swim.

As you find the floor,   your face   lifts up
    to swallow   a glassy, clear lungful
of light,   taking what you came for.

A teen
    trips
into a dive, bringing the scene   to the boil.

Boundary

Holly Corfield Carr

You tell me that depending on where we look
there are either
two hundred and thirty thousand species in the seas

or ten times that number. You stop to drink your gin
and look
over at the window where sodium vapour lamps

line up a vertical string of stars, the long rods of rain;
a sudden asterism
that perforates space. We catch each other looking

and our
    sore, slack
parallax

folds,
  crossing
our lines

  of sight, between us,
netting space
          like a ham.

and, you rose, depending
on where you stand, there
are five oceans—southern,
pacific, atlantic, arctic, indian—

or three. You see, you said,
on the worn floor of the ocean
the world's water rolls amongst
itself in one continuous change.

Still, still above sea level, we draw in dry biro
these dotted lines,
tearing ourselves on wire slung between drifting buoys.

Syncopate

Holly Corfield Carr

The rain breaks and we leave
our half-drunk drinks and a bowl
of salted, half-mouthed vowels
at the bar and stand to dance,
hastily pocketing soiled plosives

like uprooted pignuts, sweet
and pneumatised with sounds
we have heard rehearsed

by rain, our slipshod compere
whose eager patter fills in
for all the broken pieces
of our chatter, our laden
aposiopesis dampened

by timpani drumrolls,
rumbled by cold calls
that come the day after.

I hang up on each broker,
breaking up on a long
distance line, a cluster
of consonants I take
for you:

may I speak with —
a few minutes of your time
— with you in mind
— to discuss the best way
forward — debt recovery
— full disclosure — debt
free — is the home
owner at home

— best for you — may I — discuss
— home — with you in — full — recovery
— a few — free — minutes — forward

fricatives full of you

∴

I move around
    my kitchen, out of
kilter, waiting for you
to come home, as you
never will again, to talk in
those fine, dry, fireside
starts and finish
the story I'm failing to tell.
I will let you this.
    I owe you this.

Michael Casey was educated in New Ross, UCD, and Cambridge. He has worked and taught in Dublin, Cambridge and Washington DC. He has published two books and a large volume of short fiction and poetry, much of it award-winning. He contributes articles to the Irish Times and Sunday Times.

Feeling The Eclipse

The street slows as the annulus glows;
then inevitably that moment of perfect
coincidence beyond imagining or prophesy.
Despite the thin halo of light, darkness falls:
a chill descends, mist or miasma,
birds fall silent, and we stand stock still,
ash-coloured ghosts, fretful and alone,
frozen in the dull tideway light,
caught between stasis and flight.
Dumbstruck, we gaze, prone again to fate,
insignificant among marvels, perfectly
aligned in an unruly universe.

Allotment

Michael Casey

Closed, gone back to Eden.
Imagine that sign on the door
of your convenient corner shop.
But there was that clearing
surrounded by tropical plants,
palms and perfumed hibiscus,
and playful, gold-black, tigers.
Seurat and Blake chatted
on a bridge over silver water,
and taught the parakeets to speak.
But soon the gloss wore off
and the garden became an allotment
with a compost shed, for the petulant
undead with time on their hands.

Michael W. Thomas's work has appeared in *The Antioch Review, Critical Quarterly, Irish University Review* and *The London Magazine,* among others. His latest novel, *Pilgrims at the White Horizon* (Silver Age), is forthcoming in 2013, as is his latest poetry collection, *Batmans Hill, South Staffordshire* (Flipped Eye).

The gather-man

The gather-man sits
on his own side of the afternoon

leans me a smile across the table
raises demurring hands against another cup

his palms are steady as the cold
that pools under winter bridges
his eyes are garnet-bright

since he came
the days have fallen like snow

I accept it:
he is the watcher of low candles
we are preparing

there is a road between right this minute
my fingers telling the rounded heat of tea

and the fields of last panic
orphan words
my little stinks of terror

the gather-man says
he doesn't know it in miles
I don't dare not believe him.

Yesterday
he got me used to shadows—
they fear, too, must reach for their kind

showed me how lush they lie
about church porches
in sun-provoked lanes

let me hear their chatter
as they are swayed down
cartooning their ignorant owners

and there was a girl
crutch-swung

failing against the town's hill
pushing at last through a little door up top

the gather-man told
of her chair and cup, her single drawer

how echo-nests are strawed within her beams
how the hours pile fatly about her

the message tape for her phone
stays bubbled and sealed

but weather or wind
she comes half-stilting down

feet out and over the morning
a child on a carney wheel

lands in a line at the market street
dips among the roses and roses

coaxes the day into yielding up
a fresh hand of remembrance.

The gather-man leans again
brackets my fingers

tomorrow he will adjust me
to how peaks and fells live their silence
the tale of the willow's weep

now we are eye to eye
his everlasting
folds about my sputter

learn, he says,
learn that girl

Come to pass

Michael W. Thomas

He has hollowed the cellar
till the mortar ledges out
like steps to a decommissioned heaven

crates of imperishables
look on each other
forward commanders keeping a steel-grey faith

a creviced box
hides silver, gold, tumbles of yen and zloty—

who knows what stake will win
once the world folds to its last imperturbable sickness?

books on growing veg in grave-deep mulch
on teasing warmth from pinholes

lie open on duvets under plastic
breviaries to be reverenced
when sores bud thick on the skin of the age

in the street
he keeps his nose up for the odours
on the wind after next

car cuts in, man shoves round man—
tidings of night-fires
calamity taking snaps of itself
in a ringing line of visors

'Closing Down'
runs everywhere beside him—

the arse-end of a nursery rhyme
cut loose from cockle-shell and bonnet

the imperishables were tricky to come by:
blueblood and pinstripe are deep in the game

each one night nearer
he revolves down below

casts a captain's eye
over crate, book, duvet

spreads metal and coin
so they make an unbustable flush

shivers nonetheless
as a breaching chill of new weather

finds his ribs, collarbone
his tenderly defenceless neck

Daisy Bank

(The Black Country, 1961)

Daisy Bank
was an hour no day would admit to

a scuttle-through
between the big roads
with their iron ribs and gawpable collisions

cats would go there
to be left out in the rain

old girls, bred among the fiery holes
would miss buses along its perimeter

set down their despairs on a smoky wall
beside Home and Colonial baggage

old boys would staff the kerbs
all flapped apart like strutless umbrellas

never quite getting round to cross
spangles of Ypres in their eyes

the burnt-out Elementary
grew helots to be shipped

when destiny bisected time
about the business of splendour in Limerick or Benin

Princess Mary of Teck stopped there once
a mutton-chop trio was sprung from Beddows' Yard
to re-bore the axle

Perry the Tipton Slasher
finessed his murdering

in the shovel-throws of darkness
behind the Viceroy's Arms.

But a breach of sun
would always find Lane's Electrical

kiss and feather its way
round eight-disc spindles, half-shelled heads

bedizen the skin of Belafonte,
Torme, Ronnie Carroll, Matt Munro

lift their smiles beyond dentition
cherish their hinterlands: Chelsea, Tobago, Bel Air

beneath unforecast scraps of blue
Daisy Bank could close its eyes and uncurl

as the songs ascended from Lane's doorway
engaged prefab, triple-chain, exhausted cladding

forest waters
soda-winks at the uptown hour
stray curls and prodigal lipstick
gondolas rifting the dusk

Morgaine Merch Lleuad is a poet and novelist. She's worked in medical research, been a stand up comic, musician, actor, artist, and EBD teacher, and has an MA and a PhD in Creative Writing. She lectured in Creative Writing at Bath Spa and now lectures with the Open University and teaches online poetry courses for Exeter

Gag

This silence is starting to show
on my skin; this dry silence
leaches moisture, and leaves me

desiccated. I am dull with tension.
Even cruel words, even vitriol would
revive me, would stop me

shedding my defences
and allow the dust to settle.
I watch my skinflakes fall towards you

coating you with an extra
layer, another barrier between us: this
could be a vicious circle,

my involuntary ecdysis
clogging your mouth
and killing conversation.

I hope it chokes you.

History

Morgaine Merch Lleuad

works best at body heat, the warm lives of
people lived in Brownian motion, as they meet
and part, constructing symphonies, cathedrals

and cups of tea with biscuits dunked just so.
Their wardrobes and worries and how they sing
and clatter through their lives is what matters

not cool dry dates and which king ruled. The sum
of their existence is more than succession, schism
and war; the flame and frost of this lost blood uncurls

the perfect fit of complex structures. History is always
too late: it waits outside the door until the party's over;
picks out the politics, and claims that it's unchanged.

Morgaine Merch Lleuad

Homo prosaicus

I want to write stars and roses and violins
about you. But biology intrudes and
I am stuck in metabolic pathways

and the viscera of your inner workings.
Your heart isn't heart-shaped, or made of
red-shiny paper, or chocolate or sonnets: its

tough muscle squeezes dead air and sugar
and acid fat-slippery slipping through
bruise-coloured tubes. If I ate you

your gristle would stick in my teeth. When you
stretch your hot skin on me, it's not sex
but the complexity of respiration and ATP

heating the tousled sheets, and sweetness is lost
in the stink and shit of you. Murmured words
of passion aren't muse-born but witch-fingered

neurones itching with transmitters: the impulse
is not love but electrical. I trap you inside a
sparking sack of mundanity and meat:

no wonder you hate science.

pushing hands

Morgaine Merch Lleuad

i do not know what it is about you that closes
and opens

me. You push and I
fold, graceful and grateful in collapse
against you;
you pull and I follow
your hand pressing
on some private place or other –

(*nobody, not even the rain, has such small hands*)

I am not as small as I was because of the
small things:
they soothe and scare me.

Tilting towards you
off balance
I follow you with a glass
with glasses
with the glassy no-sleep stare
of the thoroughly-made-love-to
crinkled and crackling
like cellophane.

I do not know how
this happens: I

open –

you close out everything else.

Born in 1963 in West Hartlepool, **Martin Malone** now teaches in Wiltshire. A winner of the 2011 Straid Poetry Award , his first full collection, *The Waiting Hillside* is published by Templar Poetry. He is currently working on his second collection, *Failed Light And After*, as well as a collaborative collection – *Fireships* – with Jo Bell.

On Discovering the C-Word for Myself

Mother forgive me
                                        I was four
and the tang of old pennies in my clammy paw
spoke of nothing else.

I was in Columbus mode,
each day uncorking new oceans,
every morning
                          a galleon to chart new world.

My sweat-and-copper hotspot
            needed a name
                                        and none came
but this
            and
                          the hard jack
                                        of your right hand
to the side of my head.

Bigmouth Strikes Again

Martin Malone

I'm afraid I'm an open book, I say stuff,
'fess up too readily in my cups and so

mess-up in moments such as these: you
with your roman nose held high in disgust

at my latest *faux pas*. And, sweetness,
I know you are only half-joking when

you say I should be bludgeoned in my bed
for selling my Smiths ticket so I could

go see The Armoury Show instead.
But, at the time, you were only just four

and, having seen them twice before –
like a Beckett play – I felt I'd got the point.

Besides, all that mass individualism
was beginning to pall; no more than

an indie Nuremberg with cardigans
and gladioli. I'd liked Richard Jobson

longer and there was a seniority
of quiff thing going on that had to be

respected. Connected was my love for
John McGeogh's guitar which I felt –

rightly as it turned out – would not be there
for as long as cool old Mister Marr's.

So don't give me back those mix tapes, don't melt
down my old Walkman; consider them my

legacy in this retro age of legacy,
alongside these inconvenient truths,

my scratched vinyl, your gigsandtours.com.
Because here in old Camden Town,

out drinking with the hung-on-too-long
and their too-young-to-have-been-there

kids, I sense that I've moved on. Darling please,
don't make me know how Joan of Arc felt.

Butch & Sundance Ride Back Into Town

Martin Malone

That moment when I start to learn to bend:
man at the wheel of his milk-float, round done
and about to go back to the depot, son
riding shot-gun to pay for his new bike.

Then Dad goes outlaw on me, turns in
a lifetime of solid adherence, turtles
his shell of honest-John, hands back
his Sheriff's badge, joins the James Gang.

We are backing up by the Dutch Houses
when the bang jolts us. Fistful of dollars,
we've been bushwhacked. Gold top bounces
from its crate and smashes onto pavement.

Brick gatepost buckled, an instant
of recognition, that blue spark of decision:
head for the hills or hands-up confession?
Father, model for me what is right

or show me a different way. *Drive, DRIVE!*
Heavy on the reins, alias Smith and Jones,
deep in the saddle and the one thing
we've got to get is out of this business.

You can't touch him for it, he's gone; jumped in
the river before me, caught his paddle-boat.
I am twelve and I'm driving the milk-float
back into town. We are laughing all the way.

That Winter

Martin Malone

After a month of snow came the rains:
chugging against the tide up Meaburn Edge,
peering through mizzle towards High Cup Nick,
all-but-stalling in lakes on the Reagill road.

The martins' nest grew sodden and heavy;
broke its spittle moorings after the night
of gales, played mud-pies with my bedroom sill
then feasted on the garden table.

Mornings were night-black and blue with cold:
big icicles snottered the gable end,
drive time was lost scraping rime off the car,
while great tits diminished in the hard frost.

The Lyvennet heron, a leggy grey clock,
met me at the gate each day; his fish round,
pulling in at the rock below the weir,
let me know if I was early or late.

Past October, the neighbours went part-time,
became a T.V.'s blue glow, chimney smoke
or *Berghaus* dummy: muffling good mornings
through zipped-up layers of Gore-Tex and wool.

The weir's white noise was my rock n'roll;
rose and fell with the flow and one night
coughed up a tree that stuck to its palate
for seven weeks, changing my lullaby

that winter, that bloody winter.

Simon Kew has published in *Agenda, Dream-catcher, Rialto, Equinox* and lives in Nottingham.

Talking to the Vogue girl.

We want to look through your eyes into clear water.
Imagine a sea of sand, a birthday of footprints
skips across the tarmac. Red balloons - jiggling
girlish bunches say you've never been so loved,
so run to the family you deserve, kiss Parisian cheeks.
Cut to flurry of sea breeze, a certain tang of Clinique.

Furrow your eyebrows into a jealous plough,
you eye the family Austin - its sloping bonnet.
Your sister slips into a Jaguar the colour of nails,
your dress is crinkles of envy. Love and hate –
those fragile rainbows glisten like goodbye lips
to *shimmer* and *fade*.

Curl the chiffon scarf for a desert caravan where dusk
colludes with pepper kernels, Sainsbury's oily dates,
illicit sand. All night a dune is asleep in one
of Ikea's duck-down oceans and the Sahara's duvet
is wanton as your shimmering hips.

Basically, you look into a night sky where Orian's belt
is a string of stars. Loosen them, one by one: so many sisters
falling, sisters under your skin. They tuck your letters in
bathrobes, each one skitters to a rendezvous with herself.

There's a million darlings languid on their lush sofas
amazed at the couch leopard's tongue, his bedroom eloquence.
So lift your gorgeous arms, let Chanel waft elegance, yes, wave
on wave and we *pan* to the carpet's vast savannah.

Simon Kew

On this the longest day

at Eyebrook's waters dark
its silverd wavy crests
dips cleats
tiny million mountains
that glint
lisp
seen and gone
silvergreygreen scimitars
sparkle gather
ghost
collapse
and
swiftsandswallows
swerve
tilt dive
chink-
black scimitars
clouds of skittering blades
cleaving cutting
black stars
alive
fluttering
a gnat's wing-beat
over Eyebrook's waters dark

on this the longest day.

Nikki Magennis writes erotic and literary fiction. She has published poems in *Gutter, Poetry Scotland* and elsewhere. In 2012 'The Whore's Bath in Art' won the James Kirkup Poetry Competition, and Red Squirrel Press will publish her poetry pamphlet in 2014.

Burning diaries

All the shameful things
best forgotten - pink lovehearts
above every i, which teenage
creep made me gush with want

how much I hate that bitch
and how worried I am about
the shape of my breasts. Lower
down, the shame of feelings

leaking all over the classroom
and how sometimes what we cut
was not only a boy's initials scored
on our inner arm, or the reckless

and terrified inhalation of tippex
thinners, or our darkest secret
hidden near the spine in code
or lemon juice - how we longed

for safety, and someone to listen
quietly, without censure.

*

Isadora Duncan's Last Words

Nikki Magennis

"Je vais à l'amour"

Oh, to be strangled by an endless
silk scarf, while entwined in the arms
of a handsome mechanic, having waved a last
goodbye. To be carried off on a wave
of aniseed and musk, pockets full
of salt and pepper shakers, wide
open mouth a bitten, juicy plum.

In truth, how did it look,
I wonder, the fast unravel, the catch
and yank, half decapitated, eyeballs
spurting from her purpled head.
Even death is a theatre, with no fire exits.
No one will escape. No one - I'm afraid -
will applaud.

*

The Rest

Nikki Magennis

Half a dozen fillings like recovered shot
dug from the skull. A greenstick fracture
healed like a bracelet, the pelvic inlet
somewhat wide. Surprisingly broad shoulders.

Two black hooks and eyes, each grip bent slightly
open. Zips. Nails. An unsoldered ring
of half crooked keys no longer rightly
aligned for locks. A pen leaking ink.

What cracked bits of me will last, which fickle
remains end up cupped in a stranger's palm?
I'll catch the reaching fingertips, tickle
the seeker's attention, take hold their arm

and lead it to my ribcage. Show them
the slant space of my heart's whole expression.

*

Worry beads

Nikki Magennis

Torn tissues, cigarettes smoked
to the knuckle, chewed fingernails.
Days wound up in worry and hope.

A flask of holy water, gold wedding
ring, the cooker's dial turned off
twice. Thought insurance, treading

either side of the cracks. You laugh
as if I don't add up, counting the steps
from my door. But I know my part.

Saving this fragile moment. Without these
thousand small distracted prayers
we're as good as broke. Trust me. Please.

Matthew Henley was born in 1975. Between 2005 and 2008 he lived and worked in Bosnia & Herzegovina, serving as Political Advisor to the UN High Representative. He currently lives with his family in London.

Shipwreck

Stefan huddled under canvas in the belly of a life raft,
curled foetal amongst the ropes, head pillowed on damp foam,
sleeping the uneasy sleep of a traveller.

The night has the softness of a dream; there is no storm
wracking the mast, no strained tendons curled
to tame the gusted sheet, no heave of bronzed oars.

The Adriatic is aglitter with promise: the liner hums
like a hospital ward, portholes open in expectation of distance,
while white-liveried waiters serve drinks and gentle encouragement.

How entirely the future surrounds him. He shifts and turns east
to a city encircled by hills, Dzeni dressed in red
and alone as the dawn breaks, holding every light in the city.

How proud she is, fending off each proffered arm, turning down
their ministrations and strange airs, the truncated view from the window.
And when she smiles he starts, reaches right

through the walls to hold her, cradling the baby-warmth
of her back to him in sleep, feeling the whole keel
of her spine curled tight against the waves.

Alas – the wind is up, the clouds alight and then darken,
strange new gleams shark phosphorescent in the deep
borne on violet swells and lightning, a whistling howl falling

on the city and the world before it. The sea now a vast gray-green wall
of darkened spume, the deck slippery like a hand passing through him,
their craft tipped like a cup, splintered into a capsize.

The calmness of the undersea. Him alone, learning to breathe
this new beginning, studying its grammar, forming first verbs then lines
to navigate by. Filling a plastic bag with drowned words

he likes the sound of, the glitter of the lost, the out of time.
Washing plates till his fingers bleed, sleeping under tables,
working his way through the streets, he finds them

kissing farewell in the light of the morning.
She is both journey and end, he mumbles, but she can no longer hear him.
The drowned have a name, he screams.

He wakes in a soil of seawater. She has unmade the dream.

Houdini

Matthew Henley

Dry crackle of paper in the quiet patter of rain
and her new weight installed in a chair, paused
for the newness of it, the drum-tight, kicked greeting.

The Beetle slowly filled with the jewellery of home;
the wedding dress folded, a lifetime of books,
their favourite prayer laid in spidery Cyrillic.

Alma tripping over her words to explain
the loose brick for the keys, the old friend of a friend,
the long drive to the border, the last sharp left.

Hasan on the porch all angry-eyed
with the brightness of love or of violence.
I'm chained to you both but she's yours. Help me escape.

All Stefan can recall is the width of his smile
like a mimic of the guard's, how he opined
that they would have got through if they'd paid.

Look at his eyes as they glitter in the dark.
How his smile's lost its magic now it's over performed
and his laugh is a rattle, a Houdini-like fake.

The Looking Glass War

Matthew Henley

You say it's me but I say it's too soon
to bandage up what's left;
these hours are a glass through

which we seem too angry, too hurt, or too cool.
So let's not talk of love nor lying;
you say that it's me, but it's too soon.

Was it the hoped-for peace that thrilled your tongue
or the wish for something more beyond
the glassy hours we'd stumbled through?

And now when I withdraw, do
you see the lie so long maligned
that you say it's me and I say it's you?

Our country's like a paper cup, my love,
full-brimmed but temporary,
and the hours are a looking-glass lit

by old joys, cradled by the soft remove
of our midnight's mad silence. Like a sad Alice,
when you say that it's me and I say it's you,
these hours are the glass that I walk through.

The Lesson

Matthew Henley

Prisoners being counted in the chill of the schoolyard.
Hasan barely raising his eyes, ticking them off one by one,
noting buckles, collar-badges, the scuff-marks

of artillery duty, the level-eyed specific fear of the taken.
Some have holes in their boots. Others are bandaged
around the ankles or the eyes, their extremities the first

to go, to force the knees up under the chin.
Two lines are being formed beside the rusted posts
of an old goal, the clean-shaven and the Orthodox.

They meet in the penalty box, casting about
for the familiarity that has suddenly proved a deserter
in a yard only minutes from home.

He has drifted off with his satchel held high, too young for mischief.
A ghetto-blaster is playing Sunny Afternoon by the Kinks.
They're kids, someone says. *Don't do this to them*.

Stuart Pickford's only collection is *The Basics* (Redbeck Press). He lives in Harrogate where he teaches in a secondary school.

Summer Holiday

France is days away: we'll count down
place names whitened by our headlights,
the warmth of night, hope the key
under the terracotta pot will open the door.

Tonight I cuddle into your back. Scented
from the bath, you feel new. I never
know the right words but touch your neck
with the whisper, *Shall we try…?*

For a moment, I think you're asleep. *Now,*
I wonder what my answer will be? I pull
away to the cooler side so our bodies
don't touch, rehearse what I'd like to say.

I don't sigh but stare at the alarm
blinking away seconds. Later,
my son comes home with his girlfriend
from the film. They laugh, make toast.

I try to forget the holiday by asking,
Are you still awake? Yes, you reply.
In that darkness, only silence follows
until sleep takes us from each other.

Perennial

Stuart Pickford

Now you've gone, I find myself
tidying you into drawers, floral cushions
slammed in a cupboard. A paper covers
the entire table. The room steps back.

I glance at what was buried in the yard.
Punching the trowel into the soil, I rummage
through dry earth for nests of bulbs,
naked-white from being found out.

You'd crowded the bed with waxy tulips
soon trashed by wind. I liked the stonecrop,
not just its name or bitter taste.
It wasn't a weed that never seemed to grow.

If you come back, there'll be no litter
of cushions. Perhaps next spring,
you'll stare out at the yard. Should I say
only the stonecrop survived the winter?

Abigail Ardelle Zammit was born in Malta in 1976. She has had poems published in various magazines including *Orbis, Aesthetica, Freefall, The Shop, Markings* and *Myslexia*. Her first poetry collection, *Voices from the Land of Trees*, was published by Smokestack in 2007. She is currently reading for a PhD in Creative Writing at Lancaster University, her main focus being a poetic sequence set in Malta during WWII .

Shepherd Boy, 1942

This is you crashing down
the mouth of a shelter, the thud of the landing
absorbed by a tide of voices contemplating
the Mystery of an angel sidling his wing
through the Virgin's window.

This, against the drone
of Messerschmitts spurting quick blood,
the limestone dripping with sickly urgency.

And the roaring is inside you,
ripping through the bone, inside you,
the hooded echoes of bomb and blast.

You rush down without
goats and sheep. When you emerge
from the furthermost hole, you are the sum
of yourself suspended beneath your skin.

Abigail Ardelle Zammit

Rushing up to the Roof during an Air-Raid

Once you've grown accustomed
to parachute bombs scurrying
like frenzied ants, tracer bullets
raising themselves against dust, gravity,

watch yourself from the tip of a diving
fighter jet; how your head is propelled
by the possibility of demise
or the likelihood of a two-winged Junker
smiting the house into a quarry.

Surely there is enough limestone to replenish
rubble, fractured churches, or time enough
to recapture yourself at that same moment
when you are shrapnelled into the sky

Now you are picking familiar pieces:
toes, tufts of hair. Plummeting down, down.
How else would you come to know yourself.

Refugee Blues, Malta

Abigail Ardelle Zammit

Homeless, we move like dust through turgid water
and do not know the inside of our mouths
from growths on wet walls in crowded shelters.

September brings rain, brackish, choking gutters,
settling under the skin. When sirens spout
we gather, moving like dust in turgid water.

Through phantom body parts, our pain still filters.
We sweat, drench sheets, endure nights as foul
as strange growths on walls in crowded shelters.

If a foetus moves inside us, it's a shudder
of shame - that in the midst of warfare we scrounged
some joy, floating like dust through turgid water.

How can we tell a snapping cord from the patter
of a shell, of shrapnel? Our ears deafened, our mouths
mimicking the hollow growths in crowded shelters,

two years in which to starve, lose limbs, get butchered
or watch a sinking convoy struggle south,
floating through smoke, through dust, through turgid water.
Hope, the dense growth against which we shelter.

Dominic Bury lives and works in London. His poetry have been published or are forthcoming in a number of poetry magazines.

Sea Lore

I.

Despite not being a man
of the sea and trusting
a well reefed sail above the charm
of naked figureheads I gather
their hymns. I learn how fear
of ruffled water without wind
exposed wreckage, a guillemot's
wing across deck in the half-dark
leaves certain coves un-navigable.

II.

On preordained evenings I hang
mollusk necklaces, flutes carved
from mackerel bone above
my harbour facing windows
and watch: the trawler-crews
working with their patchwork of nets:
picking at dead herring as if it were
snare-bait, as if tonight one misplaced
hand could rouse more
than yesterday's catch.

III.

Patrolling Culbone beach in the eerie
gull-less calm that precedes dawn
we come across what they tell me
is evidence: half-gnawed whale carcasses
concealed with sand and Marram.
Returning with fuller light I unknot
their parables. I reveal not the sea's
catacombs, but a row of dunes
and punched through their tops
where the gristle of their flukes
had been the tail like forks
of dead hawthorn trees.

Gull Space

Dominic Bury

Before the plunge
pillared on the shear

a polka-dot
of nests.

Stray twigs, an ordered matt
of fishing wire,

a thicket of discarded
human hair.

Under the muffle
of the oceans crescendo

a pair of gannets
slump.

White and black
the slick darts

climb
the vortex's rim

toward strato-sphere
gathering gravity.

A fair lick above,
hanging on updraft

their wings
fail the air.

Folding from gull space
they needle the froth.

Hiatus

Dominic Bury

In a harbour of wind scrubbed hills
Craigmalloch anchors to the nooks
of cliffs. An ultramarine shear
of glass stretches

so thick and smooth you could click
a boulder for miles. The bitter air swells:
lifting in the seam of the dark
an imposter's pulse.

Twenty seven years and still
the crags lean in, blotting
the world from view.
The hotel where they had

in a tremor of hipbones: enmeshed
themselves, the clack of mirth
in her throat. The landscape
that vanished in an uproar of flakes.

His heart stammers, stiff legs open
like rusty hinges
he jerks forward.
He can see her breath falling

a new veil for an off white world.
He creeps nearer.
A doe in the snick of a dying moon
starts, rears and bolts.

His face drops. His shoulders shudder
and heave. One pair of footprints
coming and going – another set,
disappearing into the dawn.

Mike Barlow won the National Poetry Competition in 2006. His pamphlet *Amicable Numbers* (Templar 2008) was a Poetry Book Society Pamphlet Choice. His third collection is *Charmed Lives* (Smith/Doorstop 2012).

Heliograph

Caught there on a webcam, a figure
continents away and pixelled on a screen.
    I watch as she sorts
among debris for some small
artefact she'll recognise as home.

I can't make out her age. She stoops.
Loneliness like this has mass.
    Wherever we are
we're all too far apart. The world expands,
the more of us are lost in it.

She's bending now to a glitter
in the ash and rubble of her village, tugs loose
    a piece of mirror, tips it
this way and that so it catches the light,
an accidental SOS into the iris of the camera.

Terminal

Mike Barlow

One way I remember us is wrong-footed, thumb-fingered,
fumbling for words while the tannoy spouted like an oracle.

Then again I like to think we might have clung together
as if nothing came between us but the breath we shared.

The smell of bacon sandwiches and diesel, no last goodbyes,
last looks, just you passing like a buddhist through the gates.

And yet, up on the clifftop later, wasn't that you at my side,
the sea answering though we'd asked it nothing, the ferry

motionless while growing smaller? Your arm linked mine
as we turned for home where the door let in a draught

to rattle the blinds like a gossip's cackle and your touch,
that light touch, was suddenly gone, and the phone not ringing

deafened me. How many times did I go back to watch sea traffic,
hang out among arrivals? Or is that a trick of memory

like my mind flipping at a sock found under the bed or,
crumpled behind the toaster, a note in your scatty scrawl,

saying you'll be back late, not to wait up – evidence
if ever I should need it.

D A Prince lives in Leicestershire and London. Her first full-length collection, *Nearly the Happy Hour*, was published by HappenStance Press in 2008. A second collection is due in 2014.

As it usually does

the wind gets up about this time
sneaky with just enough tug
flicking a page or loose hair
or somebody else's sweet wrapper
tipping over shingle and stone
and half-hearted patches of sand
children claim for storybook seaside
sandcastle business
the moat always leaking and the youngest
tottering with excitement egged on
by careful! and watch it!
the tide going out or coming in
appearing to do neither

and the question's there like a cloud
miles out to sea and small
only a scrap in the sky but it'll grow
when we have to give something sorry
to its goosebumped nagging
won't take no
insists until it's covering the whole sky
and where did that come from?
newspapers flapping like flags
picnics shredded, even the gulls
pitched off the rooftops and now
the weather's really coming rough
dragging the horizon.

To

—both of you, obviously, because
singling you might risk unbalancing
the tidy stack of lives we've built up, since.

A house of cards: it only takes one breath
or tell-tale tremor (one or other hand)
or door left carelessly ajar.

So: both. Good wishes.
(Nearly neutral words.)

Love in its guises might be awkward here.

Interviews

John Gallas
interviewed by Angela France

John Gallas was born in New Zealand, came to England to study Old Icelandic at Merton College Oxford, and stayed. Worked for twenty five years with Leicestershire Student Support. Ten books from Carcanet, two from Agraphia Press (Ballad Books with Clifford Harper), two from Cold Hub Press (NZ). www.johngallaspoetry.co.uk and on Facebook.

Reading your books, the strongest impression I get is that of an irrepressible joy in language and how it sounds; is that where poems begin for you?

I think it all probably begins with an irrepressible joy in creating. This enables Looking, or maybe Seeing, which results in Ideas or Impressions for poems. What follows is the dark before the joy, for me. The first draft, the getting down of an idea into a first form that will show the way to a final version, is not joyful at all. I will do anything to avoid this intensity, which intensity, however, begins the process of the enjoyment of language. I have been known to go off on my bike, go to the pictures, go to Norfolk, go swimming, anything to put off that Big Push. But then it's born, and the best part follows : the serious tinkering, where the full play and delight of language can be fitted about the darker expression, which is Effort, of the poem. Sometimes I feel that the Completed Thing is already done, by someone or something else, and needs to be Found : when a word, a phrase, a line, a verse seem Right, I know it, which is spooky and inexplicable, except by that Platonic idea.

The energy of language that I love is also something researched, and not at all completely spontaneous. I wish I had every existing word in my soul, but I don't: consequently, with the striving for energy and joy in language inherent in my way of writing, I can hardly finish a poem without several Roget's Thesauruses, two rhyming dictionaries, and a selection of other Reference books related to the subject of the poem, in all of which can then be found the amazing, the surprising, the vital, and the Perfect word.

I also try very hard not to write, ever, a slight poem : perhaps this not altogether healthy intensity of intention also informs the vigour of the final production. The sound of a poem matters to me, especially, paradoxically, in set forms, which I use often, the sonnet most. To get the right word and the right rhythm and then, at a line's end, the right rhyme, is a triple vexation and pleasure. And I suppose a general joy-of-the-world, something that, with age, becomes simpler, and more focussed, transmits itself through language into a poem. My most recent work, a series of poems on hayfields in Rutland, a set of sonnets by a fictional rhymester from Gedney Drove End in Lincolnshire, and travel poems from Vanuatu, Rajasthan and Andalucia all have, I hope, a new luminosity that comes from the shining through of that joy, via language simpler, but, I hope, no less effective.

You've started several hares there I'd like to follow, but let's start with travel. *Fresh Air,* the first part of *Fresh Air* and *The Story of Molecule,* was all written while 'on the move' according to the back cover gloss. How do you balance that dark intensity at the beginning and the later need for reference material while travelling - how do you manage your creative drive while on the move?

Notebooks. Or, if I've forgotten pen and paper, or ridden or walked off without them, or it's raining or snowing, or writing just isn't practical, the annoying and quite alarming effort to remember the idea, line, phrase or rhyme that started the whole thing off. I remember cycling about Tonga nodding and pedalling like a rhythmic idiot trying to preserve the light, the grass, the dogs and the ideas set running after coming across an ancient stone throne in an isolated field. I expect a few what I thought of as Just Right Things flew away as I bombled along.

And the Campbeltown poems in *Fresh Air* had to be reconstructed after writing them on a piece of paper with a wet pencil and then watching the whole bloody lot disintegrate in a rainstorm in my flooded pocket. And the poem written at the top of Mount Vaea in Samoa whilst sitting on R.L. Stevenson's grave fell to bits with humidity and I thumped back down the hill reciting it until I found an old brown paper bag and borrowed a pencil from a man selling drinks on a tricycle. Usually, though, I've got something that survives, and the First Effort gets set down. Is this dark and difficult ? I think, in the case of travel poems, that comes next, meaning there's a kind of extra layer to the writing.

Back in the hut, or the Lodge or Guest House, the old black wrestling comes. I remember in Vanuatu I carried a notebook while I biked the circuit of Efate, and saw a huge tree hurling its massive seed pods onto the ground. I stopped, drew the tree, noted that I thought it looked a bit like a fairground ride, and that something about chucking away each day in what looked like a leather purse was in my thoughts, which were unaccountably, but interestingly, black(ish). Along with three or four other potential poem-stuffs, I rehearsed these as I rode along all day.

That evening, on a little guest house balcony, I did the difficult, agonising stuff (though it is quite a small poem), and got it into shape : but the final, in this case quite minimal, tidying up didn't come until I was home, with my comforting reference books – though I think I remember I changed, in the end, only one word. It's on the Carcanet blog : short, dark, rhyming, two verses. The only poem I have ever completely written to its final end is the Derry Station origami poem in 'Fresh Air', done on the train on the way back to Belfast. I still laid it out for its operation when I got home, and assembled the reference books – but nothing changed. I don't think it shows – which is interesting.

So the extra layer of creation is that notebook-plus-mental rehearsal, which is fun, then cranking up to the beginnings of the Tough Sorting, back somewhere still. Emotion recollected in tranquility with the help of paper, pens, pencils, and a head full of rehearsals.

The first four little poems in *Fresh Air* are pretty typical. The first was written, in its Tentative Shape, on a bench buried in several feet of snow ; the second on the city walls of Diyabakir next to three men asleep clutching their scythes to them beneath the huge billboard painted with Ataturk's proclamation ; the third on a coffee mat in Timaru, where I read the story in the paper ; and the last at 30,000 feet after visiting the cockpit of a flight from Heathrow to NZ. They were all Managed later. I think to leave any writing, mental or physical, too long after the scene, would be to lose the vitality that I love so much in writing, and try to convey in the poems.

The 'Ode to Autumn' was done, intentionally, as if it were a painting. I sat beside the tree, I remember it was bloody freezing, and looked at it at every word or line. 'The Mongolian Women's Orchestra' took over a year to complete. The notes were made on the spot, at a little performance in Ulaan Baatar ; they were then expanded in the guest house that evening ; rethought and rewritten on and in various buses, trains and quiet moments while still in Mongolia ; tightened and ordered and reference-booked back home ; slightly changed after recording a reading ; slightly changed after first publication; and, at last, in the state it already existed Up There in my Find Me I Am Finished complete works.

Your joy in creating is apparent in how you write about it; is this joy something you have always been aware of – or something you have discovered along the way?

Joy. Hm. It's an interesting word, but, wierdly, I think it pretty well covers what goes on behind my writing, and, I hope, into it as communication. It's something that lies deeper than fun, or a smile, or even enjoyment or enthusiasm : it can even go hand in hand with dark thoughts and gargantuan effort. The joy is still there. The easy bit is the fun of language : in that Serious Tinkering that goes on after the black labour, language can be made to sparkle and sing, or have a deep, calling chord in it that makes a poem more than approachable, even seductive. What makes it a good read, and want to be read, really.

The harder bit is that Joy : but it is there in the way that Dante's *Divine Comedy* isn't a barrell of laughs but moves inexorably and with belief towards some kind of light. And I think that might be what I'm getting at. I've already said that I often think my poems are Up There Somewhere (or sometimes Down There Somewhere), already written, and I must search for them as I work, word by word, line by line, until I capture what is there – the poem I know is Right. It doesn't take much, I suppose, to imagine the Up There, or the Down There are some place holding the joy like honey in a bucket, ready to slip out when the Done Poem descends from on high, to the page. If that sounds a bit dumb, or a bit mystical, then so be it : there is something in the creative process that *is* at once the writer's own, and something else's. How many times do novelists say that the character, or the plot, ran away with itself, made itself, took shape and ways that were not intended in the fragile conceptions they first had of what might be. It's the same with poetry. That search for the Other, through one's own abilities is, I think, both the way to that Joy, and the employment of it. You've gotta have it to get it.

If that comes through in my poetry, I'm pleased, because I guess it shows that no matter how grim or how abstruse or how apparently objective the works are, they are all managed through joy, in order to get to more. 'Molecule' is a good example: there are all the little joys (for me) of New Zealand place names, familiar beaches, my own thoughts and feelings, friends, memories, birds, plants, holidays, shops, motels and suchlike, and, holding these all together, the deeper joy of putting into sonnets what I believe about life in the form of a tale with characters.

And Molecule himself is both: genetically off-centre, a determined, if passive, denier of Evolution and all it brings, travelling amongst the variety of the earth, and thus binding the two together.

Finally, I think that this joy *can be* just something on the Bright Side. I love writing poems to make people laugh : 'The Man Who Went the Other Way Down the Road to Samarkand', the 'Origami Poems', some of the sonnets in 'The Coalville Divan' in 'Star City', 'A Complete Guide to a Few Things on Efate', for example : and this comes from the right words linked in energy, which is also joyful to do and to, I hope, read. And it can lie even in some forms that I love : the ballad, the sonnet – that possibility of the surprising, clever or neat rhyme, or word at the right time, juxtapositions that surprise, images that amaze. These are all elements of a smile.

The Story of Molecule is joyful - and extraordinary. I am interested that it is filled with so much of your 'little joys'; as a reader, I had a sense of the character Molecule taking on a life of his own in the way I have sometimes heard novelists say of their characters. Was that your experience of it? or did you know where he was going?

I think I had the plan, but did not know, and was happily surprised by, how the little character grew. Weirdly, for a creation that was made to pass along a small corner of the world without, basically, being Normal and Safe, Molecule does become likeable, even lovable, in his dissociated determination. A lot of readers have said they think he is fun, brave, even noble, sympathetic, and, also peculiarly, provokes a kind of protective Mother-Love in their reactions.

This is *exactly* the point. If it is possible to make a plan to create a series of events to illustrate something, and then, in the creative process, the Human side of the character develops (in this case partly because he does not, or refuses to, develop) gains sympathy and becomes something the reader wants to know what happens next to because they sort of care about it, and him, then you have got the two levels of Writing and Engagement that any poet would want in telling a story in verse, or verses.

Mostly, when it comes to literature, I retreat from the idea that a work is About Something (and, therefore, Relevant, or not) because it makes for a kind of neat dismissal, oh I know what's that's about, it's about Belief, bing bang done. That means that the actual process of the work

95

is thought to be the servant of something Higher.

Now although 'Molecule' did have a This-Is-About-Escaping-Evolution idea behind it, the fact that readers remember the details – probably because, coming from my own experience, I have tried to make them vivid and thus engaging – the little scenes, the minor characters, the being knocked off his bike, the being caught by the Police, the encounter with sacred waters, the encounter with the bride, with the deer, with the motel occupants - means that the kind of *level* of the particular rises against the *level* of the big idea behind, and makes them more equal. Actually, I hope, in 'Molecule', that the particular completely outweighs the theoretical.

Poets that tell stories have always to try and find this balance, or imbalance, to be effective. Of course, Chaucer does it perfectly. His Canterbury Tales are often very clearly 'moral' or 'About' something, but what you remember (also ?) and delight in most is the detail – what the characters are wearing (whether that is tied-in relevant to any metaphorical purpose in the Tale or not), the horses, the pokers, the ships, the chickens, the fruit trees and the Noble Knights. Critical reaction will tell you that *every* detail in Chaucer is somehow Relevant to his higher purpose, which, of course, is bloody good – for them and him – but it does not mean at all that that is the way a Tale is read and enjoyed. I hope that 'Molecule', in the writing, and this is probably the bit that 'gets away' in your question, becomes more delightful – in both himself and all the things that go on around him – than Relevant : though, of course, my Thoughts About Life, even my One Big Thought About Life, are in there, like a pattern you can only see from an aeroplane, where you wouldn't really want to be that much, or for that long. Crabbe's 'Tales' and 'The Borough' / 'The Parish' do the same thing. Soaked with local detail and carefully written and developed, these little narratives are often highly moralistic, or illustrative of a Point (pregnant young country girls, how love transforms perception, the behaviour of clerics), but would not now be read, rather than studied, for that.

They survive, easily to my thinking, because of their vividness, because of that balance having been found, that makes a reader what to know what happens, to delight in 'imitation', to have belief and fellow-feeling in and for the characters involved, and just have a bloody good read. Hardy has a Big Idea, which *on reflection, after reading,* casts a shadow on the wonderful events and characters of his novels; but the reading is as vivid and human as it could be. Tolkein, often dismissed as A Man With One Idea, is as popular as can be. Why? Because his Great Idea (whether it be Good vs Evil, Home vs Adventure, Rural vs Industrial) is represented in deeds and characters and scenes so absorbing that, in this case, they become an actual *part* of the Idea, which both fades and remains ever-present.

Sorry to go on, but I think that if a poet tries to write a narrative, and that is deeply unfashionable at the moment, all these things have to be taken on board. 'Molecule' has its Idea : does mankind bobble along doing what Evolution nudges or drives him or her to, having all the Right Reactions and doing all the Right Things (be born, be looked after, sow some wild oats, get hitched, have children, look after them, let them go, wither and die) – all

96

these things, perhaps, actually being quite out of the actual control of an individual, and urged on by the chemicals that Evolution has developed (babies are cute, look after them: orgasms are fantastic, make children : old people are useless, read the paper every day) – or, well, simply, Not. Molecule chooses, or simply develops as a, NOT. The other characters in the sequence deal with the realisation that Molecule inspires in them, that there is another life, which may not be Righter or Wronger, but has different actions and purposes and opportunities, in their different ways, depending on how brave, stupid, unsure, hidebound or receptive they are. Dad, Nana, Wig and Steff, DS Baigent, Witi Jones – all are affected, all react.

And this idea must be turned to a story. I hope that 'Molecule' does that, and if it does, it is entirely due to the 'not knowing what will happen' while the writer is writing. Not that I did not know how things would go, actively: but I could not know how, humanly, Molecule himself would grow in the context of the many things that go on around him, simply by being there. So I've put him here, there, and everywhere, in the north of the South Island of New Zealand, and let him, if it's not a stupid word, 'become.'

The end of the story is particularly relevant to this. The combination of story, character, idea, and even writing technique and what it can 'mean' here combine at Molecule's exit. Similes break down, the comforting comparisons that make Nature bearable in literature disappear, that cosy companionship we think we share with trees and fishes, sunsets and seascapes is denied, the demands of Evolution thus become nakedly isolated, and, here, of course, refused, and Molecule goes into the bush, which takes him without meaning. Wow.

There are Ideas all over the show : but it's the out-of-control development that gives the sequence its life. In sonnet 107, the last, family and friends pass quietly through the beauties of the world in a kind of anaesthetic pursuit of the Bad Boy. How much you hope they will find him, for his own and their sakes, might be a good measure of your response to the Idea – but you have got to the end, because you wanted to read on, enjoy the story itself in all its real detail, and put the book down, I'm hoping, with both a smile and a Thoughtful Expression.

"a smile and a Thoughtful Expression" is a good way to end any reading. Thank you for your time; I'd like to finish by asking what's next? Do you have a project you're working on?

Blimey. Yes. Rather. I'm editing *The Complete Poems of Isiah Woodhouse*, which consists of eight sonnets, written about 1910 (I think), found in a house in Gedney Drove End in Lincolnshire. They were typed up by someone on an old typewriter in the 60s. They are quite something : dark, a bit mad, lovestruck in the knock-over-the-headest way possible, beautifully constructed, and tantalising – can't find him in any Census documents, and the hints of suicide and withdrawing from the world are many.

I've just finished a full-length 21st Century Dante entitled *The Little Sublime Comedy*, in which the Poet, who is Me, is led by Beckett (until things become too cheerful, about half way through Purgatory, or The Better Place) through the Three Domiciles of the Dead. That's taken about three years.

97

I've just submitted my one-and-only ever novel (I just promised myself to do it once), *Bush* to a few folks in New Zealand : it's a terrible tale of revenge, betrayal, gold, hideous violence and a bloody good laugh in the NZ goldfields at the end of the nineteenth century. That's taken a while as well.

I've tidied up a collection called *Pacifictions*, made up of all the poems I wrote in Tonga, Samoa, Cook Islands, NZ, Australia, Tahiti, Hawaii, Nolfolk Island, Bali and Fiji in the last few years – a bit more 'Fresh Air' really, but with a warmer clime ; and they're to be published by Cold Hub Press (NZ) with some pictures by the print-maker Sarah Kirby, who's from Leicester.

Rhymes With Hay, a bunch of poems written while cycling about the Rutland wheatfields last summer, is coming out from Pig Hog Press soon(ish), also with Sarah's picture as a cover. And my present task is *The Rotoiti Diwan*, a collection of little prose-poems, nothing longer than 20 lines, that have characters and words and events and ideas that run in a strange repeating pattern throughout. And lastly, I'm collaborating with my brother on translations for Carcanet of the six long and bloody impossible poems written by Jean Genet. They will, I think, be 'versions', as they are so allusive, echoey, complex, wilfully obscure and often Not Very Nice, that they can't be given anything literal, as choosing one way to do it precludes so many others. That's the challenge for the empty moments. Which are few, so it all might take a good while.

In between, I'll be off on my bike, going home to NZ (another winter), swimming up and down, and looking for The Next Thing, or waiting for it to hit me.

98

Driving behind the chaff tractor

Content thus slow, my quiet mouth agape
with minor awe, I feel my dusty lens
receive the pattered storm of useless chaff,
and blink. The sun-splash weaves
along the falling leaves.

And in this guttering, spermatic light
it seems the seed of some unfruitful Adam
swims in barren show against the glass,
golden and unblessed :
how sweet is second best.

You coupled children, couched in beds of wheat,
where generations thrive and dreamt-of summers
lie in store – enjoy your harvest. I
will rattle home behind
this tractor, and not mind.

99

The Complete Guide to a Few Things on Efate, Vanuatu

John Gallas

a. the Rain

the Rain on Efate
does not move.
Biking through it
with surprising bursts of speed
can be very refreshing.

b. the Long Comma Bird

the Long Comma Bird goes
tooooo-whop, tooooo-whop,
punctuating, on cloudy mornings,
The Tree With Hanging Pods.
Together they look out
upon grey pages of bays
from trim slopes.

c. the Tinsel Bird

the call of this bird
resembles
a little rope of tinsel
dropped.
I have observed its shadow
somewhere skiusmi also
bouncing separately
between the side lawn
and the gas-driven shower.
What does it all mean ?

d. the Exactly White Rooster

This enchanting creature
is a Glacier Range Toyota 4WD pickup
with silver ornamentallations
that has just driven away.
It is said that the lingering hooter
has the power
to destabilize
the Gliding Goddess Flower.

e. Kindness

this enviable quality
was preserved here
by some
inconceivable bloody turn of events
concerning Gondwanaland
and the Trans-Siberian Railway.
Halo, says Prime Minister, Yu orate ?
to which reply is Yis, tata.

f. the Tree With Hanging Pods

Lest we forget our wasted days
the Tree With Hanging Pods displays
the lot, aloft like leathern purses
withered by Ancestral Curses.

Once these trees went round and round,
bombing on the golden ground
the Seeds of Immortality,
but, ah, it matters not to me.

g. nice Smiling Dogs

the original Smiling Dog
was knitted by a kindly old Palm Tree
long ago in a time
of universal love
it says here.
Some say
it is a hopelessly corrupted text,
but I, who once was rabid,
hold it to be true,
for one of the dear little fellers
is wagging up the road with me now.

h. the Pigs of Fila

the Pigs of Fila
came out of the Nostril of God
to promote the avoidance of sin
by their bloody extreme Sloth.

they are all distension and tits,
they must be stoned, brothers,
and their extremities affrighted,
that they bear away evil into the bush.

And, as is written, hooked squealy and blood
they will be stuck and ate in the snot greenery,
for the bastard wages of sin, though it be
God's gift that they smiled in, is death.

i.Song of the Private Buses

sherpherds
why worry
Men in Blacks
carry yumi home
without
Lord
I am
nothing
Digicel

j. theWalking People of Mele-Maat

they wend a sort of woven thing
mostly they wear shorts and sing

hither and thither up and down
uzhly not and sometimes town

God could make a mat or two
mostly brown with bits of blue

k. the Gliding Goddess Flower

When whisp'ring souls their cold quietus make,
and gentle forth to meet the Big Go Wai,
a Goddess Flower falls, its wee white bell,
sounding, stamen-tongued, its petal knell
unto the lapping earth. Pretty, eh ?
Tonight the darkling branches softly shake.

Jo Bell
interviewed by Angela France

Jo Bell is a working poet and former director of National Poetry Day. A festival programmer and performer Cheshire Poet Laureate, Glastonbury Poet in Residence and now the UK's Canal Laureate, she is working on a collection to follow *Navigation*, and on an hour-long performance piece about life on the waterways for touring in spring/summer 2014.

Firstly, congratulations on becoming the first Canal Laureate. What, if any, difference has this made your your life as a poet?

Thank you. A commission like this is an immense opportunity. It's a gesture of trust from the Poetry Society and the Canal and RiverTrust. I get paid to write about a subject I *want* to write about, with a great deal of freedom. It gives a useful sense of my worth in other's eyes; and I get PR and organisational support from my sponsors.

This great opportunity also brings to the fore the self-doubt that all writers carry. I sit down to write on the subject that means most to me, and here come the goblins with their little placards: *What if you fail? What if you fail with all these people looking at you?* The greater exposure brings - well, greater exposure. My way of life as a boater is so essential to me that I feel both evangelistic and intensely private about it. There's a feeling of responsibility - as if I have this one chance to communicate everything about canal life on behalf of everyone who lives it. That's spurious. We can only ever write as well as we can write at this moment; and it's a nonsense to wait, in a perfect vacuum of inactivity, to evolve into a better writer. *Don't get it right, get it written* as the saying goes.

You are one of the busiest poets I know; you seem to be always travelling around the country, giving workshops or performances, organising and promoting events. How do you manage your own writing? Do you snatch time where you can or are you disciplined about setting aside time to write or think about it?

All that work and travel is an elaborate mechanism for procrastination. I do schedule time to write; I also schedule time to clean the bathroom and do my tax return, but the end result is the same – a blank page and a guilty face.

I have had some success with deadlines imposed by friends – like Max Wallis whose 'something every day' blog got me writing every morning because he needed a poem a day from me for the blog. But the truth is my most successful poems are written on the spot, at great speed, immediately after the incident that provoked them. So, as frilly and poetical as it sounds, I have to write when it comes, and write fast, chasing the muse down the corridor before she makes off with the goods. I may work on something for a long time afterwards – but like Norman McCaig, who said you could write a poem in the time it takes to smoke a cigarette, I have to get the bones of the thing on paper straight away. In fact, when I am stuck, I think of McCaig, set my timer to 11 minutes (the time it takes to smoke a fag) and see how far I can get. The urgency often produces good things; but never, alas, as good as McCaig.

Does the muse ever get away down the corridor – are there times when you can't write? If there are, how do you deal with it?

She gets away more often than she should.
I admire those people like David Morley, whose prodigious talent is matched by his self-discipline. But if I try to force it, the work sounds stilted. And what, in any case, is the value of a forced poem? If you don't have anything to say, then keep your mouth shut. When you have something to say, then make damn sure you say it well, and in your own strong voice, and with conviction. Far too many poems are published which have no reason to exist; they are just lists or tedious personal recollections with no real meaning, or technically competent efforts with no blood in them. Martin Malone and I had a project to find poetry in which one could see 'shit, spunk, and rapture' and that's what I want. Something visceral and honest. Self-exposure without self-indulgence.

How do I get over my little blockages? Usually by sucking up energy from someone else's artistry. Live music in particular can kick-start my own creativity. Brilliant poetry reminds what poetry can do, and how generous it can be in offering something valuable to the reader. Bad poetry too can spur me into writing – Jesus, if s/he can publish this then I can do better! And also, that feeling that perhaps I do have things to say that can be of use, or that I have a worthwhile insight into – canal life, and what it means to live it, for instance.

You mentioned a project with Martin Malone, and I know you have collaborated with others at different times, such as on the show Riverlands, with storyteller Jo Blake Cave. How does collaboration affect your creativity? Is it a benefit or a pressure?

Both. A real collaboration should challenge all parties involved, and result in work which is more than the sum of its parts: work which one would never have generated alone, and which may possibly be diminished when seen out of context. It requires trust and generosity. Jo Blake Cave and I pushed each other in directions that neither of us would have explored, had we stayed in our comfort zones. Riverlands, an hour-long piece about the River Nene, surprised us both; my poems became more narrative and her narratives more poetic. Likewise my current project 'Erasures' (http://www.morethanerasure.tumblr.com/), led by Kevin Reid with George Szirtes and others. It's a cumulative collaboration – Kevin gives us an altered text from an Oliver Wendell Holmes book and we create a visual and textual response. The method and tweet-length form are forcing me into some odd corners. Sometimes writers should be backed into a corner to see if they can write their way out of it.

My happiest collaboration was part of the 'Companion Stones' project (http://www.artsinthepeak.co.uk/cs/home/home1.htm). Artist Kate Genever, poet Ann Atkinson and I devised two poetry stones for the Peak District. The poems and sculpture forms react to one another, and our two poems share a phrase. Ann and I became close friends as we worked out how our stones should 'talk' to one another. She died last year but that collaboration, literally written in stone, will outlive us both. The other one I'm really proud of is the lock gate near Huddersfield where artist Peter Coates has carved my words into the wood (http://www.locklines.org.uk/). Good collaboration is about working together, not showing off to each other.

Collaboration, and how people work with it, is interesting when so much poetry writing is a solitary activity. How do the collaborations start? Do you come up with something from discussions with the other person/people, or are you ever in a position of collaborating with others you haven't known before?

It's a bit like dating, actually. Sometimes your eyes meet across a crowded room and you just get on with it, and sometimes there is a clever matchmaker involved. Either way, it won't work without the right chemistry and a willingness to take risks. Jo Blake Cave and I were brought together by a third party, and both were wary until we met - when we hit it off straight away, and knew it would work.

Collaborations that don't quite work are valuable too. Like any mistake, they show you your own strengths and weaknesses, or unearth strong reactions which you hadn't expected. I'm all for working with other art forms too, not just writers - so long as you create something collaborative, and not just a response to someone else's work. I'm suspicious of ekphrastic poetry for instance, because it can turn into an elaborate caption for a self-sufficient painting. Alastair Cook's *filmpoems* reverse this brilliantly, making new films in response to written work; and Longbarrow Press is always encouraging poets to work with film-makers and painters. I'm hoping to work soon with a very talented young flautist, and a composer. Watch this space. Oh, and I ought to add that my current project CUT will include commissioned pieces from Ian Duhig, Liz Berry and Ian McMillan - not exactly collaboration but at least a sort of anthology!

All of these collaborations bring exposure, which you are already experiencing through the Canal Laureateship; it seems to me that the poetry world is coming on board your narrowboat, rather than you (and your writing) venturing out from it, if that makes sense. Is this a new form of pressure? What effect does it have on you and your poetry?

The world in my narrowboat? Yes, it gets a bit crowded in there. It's interesting, working out what to tell and how, because there is a culture and a jargon to boating life which is hard to communicate without sounding fey. I feel more exposed writing about canals than I do about anything else, oddly. I feel a (spurious) responsibility to represent life on the waterways without caricaturing it or making it sound quaint. The canal community is resolutely unromantic - emptying a chemical toilet will do that for a person - and there is not a strong tradition of poetry. So my poems may bore the boaters who aren't interested in poetry AND the poets who aren't interested in boating. You just have to tell your truth and hope that others will recognise glimpses of their own within it. If they don't then you're not connecting with others, you're just wanking. And we get enough of that in poetry, surely!

If the canal community is 'resolutely unromantic' and without a tradition in poetry – how have they responded to having a laureate? Linked to that question is another – what do you think (or hope) can be achieved by a canal laureate?

It hasn't been a universal welcome. A lot of boaters and canal enthusiasts are committed conservationists – the very people who rolled up their sleeves and lobbied hard to save our canals – but some apply the same great energies to opposing any sort of change. Also, it's a largely vernacular culture which generally values practicality and community work, and is suspicious of 'art'. The Locklines project which put poetry on four locks across the Midlands and North, for instance, took some flak. Most people love it, but don't say so until they meet me – the critics are always louder and more public. But we have to create a wider appreciation of the canals amongst those who don't know already what a gem we have, in the long grass at the back of the city centre. That's what a canal laureate might help to do. The waterways are worthy of occasional good, contemporary interventions – not just well-intentioned, poorly-executed piecemeal projects. We have thousands of miles of water and there is room for the odd piece of poetry which honours and respects the canal in a new way. I try to remember the old saw – 'Any fool can criticise, and many of them do.'

At the beginning of this, you said, about your life as a boater, that you 'feel both evangelistic and intensely private about it'. I wonder whether the feeling of privacy makes your work as Canal Laureate feel riskier than poetry you've written before; is there a point when achieving 'wider appreciation' of the waterways could encroach on the life you value and the poetry that springs from it? And to finish with – what's next for you?

Well, I won't be entirely dedicated to the canals – I still write rather strongly about relationships and sex, which is perhaps what I do best (in poetry, I mean!) But the laureate post has made me think differently about exposure in poetry. Canal poetry is risky in that I can get it factually wrong. I'm trying to write a piece about a canal lock; the sense of both explaining it to a non-boater, and doing justice to its simple elegance for boaters, without boring all of them shitless.... It's a quandary. But it's a first-world problem, after all.

A wider appreciation of the waterways could never encroach on the life I value, in fact absolutely the reverse. The very life of the waterways is at stake in coming years. If we don't get more people using the canals in all possible ways – for boating, walking and cultural regeneration – then they will decline again and my way of life will be impossible. But above all, I must not romanticise it. The gas just ran out for instance, and I need to go and change the cylinder.

Severn

Jo Bell

Don't take my lightness lightly; there is gravity
behind it. This slow fix, this great meander
that supplies the land's great wants:

this fluid strength is what we borrow,
what we lean against when love inhabits us.
It alters when it alteration finds, alright;

and so it should. There is no ever-fixèd mark.
The bark's the thing; the dot that battles tides
and if the water lets it, makes its small unlikely win.

Jo Bell

Boat

Tonight you moor at Tixall Wide beneath the giddy bats.
A heron tries one leg. The boat is tethered,
browses between bank and channel.

In dry dock once, you saw her settle on the bostocks,
wondered at her bulk; that welded self
as helpless as a brick. Her power's in suspense.

You don't need to travel far. You're always home.
There's comfort in the play of rope;
slack and tight, there and back.

Philosophy

Jo Bell

Because of the spaniel splashing in
and back along the towpath

shaking a chandelier of drops
onto the slack old man in a white cloth cap

who waves at Anne-Marie;
because of Anne-Marie

who threads her long dark boat
through eyes of stone-arched bridges

past the beetles busy at the water's edge,
the duckling beetling around its own meniscus;

because of the papoosed baby
swaddled and wanting, surprised by everything;

the man beneath the papoose
so surprised by love;

the little girl in the red-flowered dress
seeing her first duckling,

the duckling in its tabby feathers
seeing its first little girl;

the moorhen fussing by its soggy nest,
the cyclist with the mud flecks on her jolting bust,

the silly birds shouting their tangled territories,
the boaters frying bacon in their galleys,

the lean-legged runner in his baggy shorts
and cattle, solemn in their drinking holes;

because the sunshine brindles all the bridges,
coats the day like custard on a spoon;

because beyond this bank the streets are
pink-paved, poppy-spotted, heavy with may;

Nothing is worth more than this day.

I will lift up mine eyes to the hills

Jo Bell

We make our own winters. *Take the valley*
or the ridge, depending on conditions
says the book. The hills are locked in snow
and I will walk from Mam Tor, shivering, to Barker Bank.

The views are clear and treacherous, the sky
an unstoppable blue. Either road, the land
will carry me unnoticed, as the river bears a boat.
I'll walk the ridge today. I'll take my kite.

Reviews

People Who Like Meatballs
Selima Hill
Bloodaxe, £9.95

This is Selima Hill's thirteenth collection and sixteenth publication. Rather unsurprisingly it was shortlisted for the Forward Poetry Prize 2012 as well as the Costa Prize. Having previously been shortlisted for the Forward in 1997 with *Violet* she has also twice been shortlisted for the T.S. Eliot Prize and has once won the Whitbread. For those unfamiliar with her work it is clear that her output is consistent and well received.

I believe Hill to have one of the strongest voices in contemporary British poetry in terms of distinctiveness. Noted for her surrealism, humour, gender politics and oftentimes eerie tone, Hill has delivered a strong and cohesive collection that carries with it traits to be found in her previous work while still pushing forwarding and striking new ground. Hill often writes in sequences of poems.

The collection is made up of two sequences. The titular, 'People Who Like Meatballs' is about the humiliating demise of a romantic relationship. The second, 'Into my Mother's Snow-Encrusted Lap', is about a 'dysfunctional mother-child relationship'. The first sequence contains much sharp honesty and yet it is from this directness that unexpected humour often emerges. In 'Arithmetic' Hill writes:

> *...I'd rather be doing arithmetic in the woods*
>
> *than having sex with you which I find distressing*
> *whereas being bored is easy and boring and nice*
> *but having sex with you is just distressing.*

The frank and seemingly flippant tone is immediately funny. However, the repetition of 'having sex with you is just distressing' actually forces the reader to re-confront the word 'distressing'. In fact, as the last line of the poem, it is where Hill leaves the reader. However, after reading this and reconsidering the title, it is possible to find further humour still in the 'arithmetic' of the statement giving the speaker's voice a sense of control over the situation.

Throughout the sequence Hill employs the recurring image of an elephant. Sometimes it is the focal point of a poem as in 'The Elephant Is Much Too Big to Boogie'. Here the elephant represents a comforting constant, Buddha-esque in his permanence and childish in his simplicity:

So ponderous and dim, he just stands there,
inert not with inertia but with love!

Other times the elephant works to support a larger theme or to advance an element of plot as in 'Snow White Katerinas':

I want to be an elephant and not
the tiniest and most something little something
it's ever been God's privilege to ruin.

Here Hill considers size and status in relation to notions of power. Her blunt tone is assured as well as playful and the directness of her language is often so alarming it starts to take on the surrealism of much of her imagery. I consider this to be Hill at her best.

The second sequence, again a blend of humour and unease, offers the reader a number of poems that inhabit the language of fairy tales to eerie effect. In the title poem of the sequence Hill writes:

Into my mother's snow encrusted-lap
I throw my little ping-pong ball – but no,

she doesn't throw it back, she's much too busy
sharpening her snow-encrusted axe.

The use of rhyme supports the childish voice while the imagery is surreal and sinister. The layout is also interesting in terms of its near symmetry between stanzas: as though representing the synergies and also the separate-ness of the mother and child. There are a number of these throughout the sequence working to provide a structure as with 'My Mother's Yard'. In the second stanza Hill writes:

My mother's in the shed chopping wood.

Pity us. We don't know what to say.

These statements are deceptive in their initial simplicity. However, as one considers the meaning of 'us' the stanza opens up. Does the child have a sibling? Are the mother and child the 'us'? Or perhaps, the reader and the narrator are 'us'? Coupled with the violent imagery and the rhythm reminiscent of a swinging axe the overall result is, again, both funny and shocking.

If you have not yet experienced the delights of reading Hill then please do. This is a really excellent collection and it would not be a bad place to start if unfamiliar with her. To those of you who have visited her work before this is the perfect excuse to return. This collection brings together classic elements of Hill's repertoire while also advancing them: her outlandish hyperbole, her overturning of cliché, her brassy tone, her shocking and hilarious imagery. It's a master-class.

Kate North

Eighteen Poems

Simon Jarvis

Eyewear Publishing, £12.99

Handsomely bound in hard covers sturdier than some of the walls in my house, Simon Jarvis' *Eighteen Poems* is a lavish production in every sense. Despite the prosaic title, it is swarming with ideas, memorable phrase-making and displays a mastery of the long line.

Jarvis has a lyric gift, as evidenced in 'Lessons and Carols', a meditation on Christmas in Cambridge where he is Professor of Poetry and Poetics at the University. We join him as 'The ring road rests, and frost settles over the meadow.' With its shades of light and dark, he establishes his Byronic credentials as he takes us on a journey around the twilight city. This long opener seems to be a treatise against commercialism - against the shops that line the streets and the objects we gifts we buy and give away as expressions of love. He considers '–how deeply they bury their spirits inside us and sing to return' and marvels at our emotional investment in them. He examines the peculiar transaction we conduct at Christmas, in which we translate currency into inanimate objects which we give in exchange for love. Striking phrases abound; he observes how 'Each glittering package/wishes to be a Cathedral imprisoning heaven', using this personification and attractive hyperbole to underline the ridiculous expectations we place on these things. However not all his learning is lightly worn, and phrases such as 'transvalued inertia' and 'habitual prosopopeias' occasionally jar rather than enhance these poems. No doubt a brilliant mind is at work here, but such prosody threatens to undermine the lyricism.

The opening line of 'Night Office' is one of the best I've read this year: 'Every last person in this book is dead/including me.' It would be a wonderful first line for a novel, and it's not a bad one for a poem. Its directness is also welcome in a book that more than occasionally becomes obscure. It is another peon to winter and 'the snow-transfigured city.' While Jarvis' approach is often wildly original, his poetic themes are familiar, watching 'flake after flake of trembling distant snow' and how 'The night/welcomes and hides them . .' He pursues ideas and thoughts prompted by these images - how black text dissolves into the white page. There is a great intimacy and delicacy as the poet becomes somnambulant, lulled by the slow rhythms of the night and the snow and language itself shifts and falters.

Like John Ashbery, Jarvis is not afraid to be self referential or to suddenly depart from his subject to reflect on the poet's dilemma; the quality of his work and his reader's expectations 'These lines of verse . . ./They have no descant, lack that holy smoke. .. /There is no point, no terminating joke.' There is also an ongoing struggle between music and the spoken word, a crisis perhaps as to which holds the greatest beauty, until it reaches a resolution of sorts:

A different line is running in my head;
it has no music; it is spoken, clear.

Jarvis' work is in constant conversation with itself; worrying about what it should and shouldn't look and sound like; what its subject should be. Should it be functional or decorative? 'I strip down/each needless colour' and 'clip each needless word' he asserts, and yet his poems are effusive and richly detailed: these bold claims about poetic austerity appear in the same poem as this luminous description:

So the electric candles, iridescing,
cast their imagined glances on a neck
whose lovely owner bends and dip.

However these contradictions create a poetic tension that binds this collection together than one that threatens to pull it apart.

The shorter poems, when they arrive are something of a relief, but are no less baffling. 'Colloquium' begins:

Ten miles below the polar ice
exists a rock that praises Christ

It displays a formal gift, and a tightly wound concision; the phrases are memorable, but the meaning is tantalisingly obtuse, suggesting a thought perhaps about the relationship between the Earth, God and man. Once again, personification of inanimate objects brings the world to life; gives voice to the universe. The rock: 'grumbles for its daily bread./It is unquestionably dead.'

This is not a collection for a single sitting; there is a density of thought and image which requires time to consider, but it rewards repeat visits. For every complex construction, difficult word or convoluted idea, there is Jarvis offers compensation in lines of generous assonance and breathtaking lyrical beauty;

So into colourfast blossoms of damp and somniferous poppy
ometimes the midnight will drop an invisible dream

Jarvis perhaps is unclear himself which path he should take: one of lucid simplicity (as is the short epiphany, USA, about a man in a car at dusk, alone with the world) or whether to dive headlong 'Down to the sugar vertex' of Persephone, a brilliant, formal triumph that could equally be considered foolish, rarefied, self indulgence. Yes, it is full of 'pretty excitements' but equally 'this paragraph so far (is) imprisoned in metaphors.'

Eighteen Poems is an exhilarating journey into the poetic consciousness, the hyper stimulation of an overactive mind and we find ourselves in the hands of an unusually gifted formal lyricist. However it is just as possible to feel like you have dropped down a rabbit hole of unimaginable depth, darkness and complexity. Jarvis is unashamed in his use of difficult vocabulary; he travels to the far reaches of the English language where 'noise is collected and hurled/ triskaidekaphobic to gather us into its fine/series of thoughts.' Is there an element of plain showing off in this unapologetic approach, an academic snobbery, or is he merely challenging us to go with him into an intellectual and aesthetic voyage into the unknown?

There are moments of almost Shakespearean grandiloquence and ambition in *Eighteen Poems*, but the danger is that these labyrinthine, Byzantine constructions obscure meaning: 'where all such messages remain unopened.' While there is jaw dropping mastery on display here, one wonders whether a paring back, a more sociable approach would open Jarvis work to a wider readership? I suspect he knows this too; for example there is genuine power (ironically) in the simplicity of Final Demand, where the power is lost:

The switch is broken.When I press
a click comes back, and nothing else.

The darkness grows around me

The use of sound and silence, the onomatopoeic percussion, is highly effective, as we can also hear in the poem 'Erlkonig':

Each quick kiss
his soles click on stone seems to award
new victories in syllogism.

Did we really need the final line or is this constant need to deduct meaning from every sound, murmur and flicker of light the duty of the poet and a necessity of the human condition? Reader . . you decide.

Christopher James

Fresh Air and The Story of Molecule

John Gallas
Carcanet, £12.95

There's an odd passage of prose wedged between the 'Fresh Air' and 'Story of Molecule' halves of John Gallas's latest collection, which purports to describe his recovery from an operation on a badly torn muscle. "I awoke in the Waking Up Room" he writes, "holding hands with a nurse who informed me that I was the smilingest person she had ever seen wake up in the Waking Up Room. I was surprised. How happy could a person *not* be upon discovering they were alive and mended after Death and Destruction?"

I can believe it. I've seen John Gallas read only once before, in London, but he struck me as pretty smiley. Even reading bits from *The Song Atlas,* the book of world poetry he edited for Carcanet in 2002 – some of which were pretty grim –

he retained a sort of Antipodean perkiness.

The Fresh Air section positively radiates good humour. From the first pages Gallas is determined to make us look at the world – *really look*; take in the colours and the shapes as if we'd never seen them before. Personally, I can't think of a better purpose for poetry than Coleridge's vision of it "awakening the mind's attention from the lethargy of custom, and directing it to the loveliness and the wonders of the world before us." I suspect Gallas agrees.

Thus, in 'Four Thoughts from Abroad', the collection opener, we admire the sky in Porvoo, Finland ("the cloud pulled thin, / nearly-torn white, and grey for its shapes, / flat, low and yellow behind the church roof"), move swiftly to Diyarbakir in Turkey ("When the sky turns red, and the star sails into the turned moon's curve") and come to rest somewhere above South Asia ("Tiny golden detail. / ... Lagoons and inlets, syrup-twists in rivers, / liquid land and light-loop flicks. / Here and there, drops of lacquered milk"). Amazingly, Gallas keeps up this inventiveness, this rapid-fire scene changing, over the next 191 pages.

Now, I'm loath to accuse anyone of being a postmodernist, you understand. In much the same way I'm loath to go on about someone's B.O. There's nothing wrong with it *as such*. It's just not a very nice thing to have pointed out. However, it does have some laudable aspects. An appreciation of playfulness, for example. Who doesn't like playfulness? Well, most postmodernists, it seems, judging by the number of po-faced hymns to humour and irony constructed in unreadable, industrial-strength prose. Genuine playfulness requires a light touch, which Gallas has. I don't know if he'd call himself postmodernist, or perhaps just postmodernish. But I'd suggest that, if PoMo is to mean anything, it should look something like this:

enter the Mongolian Women's Band
with
the years,

whose music, theirs and theirs, like language learned,
inevitable, red and super-sound
outplays the days the days that made it mine

and beauty beauty adds to it – its stir,
its wink, its melt, and anything that shines –
this is The Horse that Overtook the Wind.

'Three Poems Written in Mongolia'

Or perhaps this:

Suddenly, from a night-ript gash,
this yellow shockthing yells into my eyes:
all-electric birdie, cackling, house-size,
chinglechingle, flickerfun and flash,
its glassmouth open wide,
nothing but yellow inside
and a brass din.

'Two Norfolk Beach Poems'

As this demonstrates, 'Fresh Air' is both formally and linguistically innovative. Gallas employs a range of traditional and novel verse forms, and coins neologisms with abandon. One poem includes a parallel txt msge; another – 'A Sonnet for My Cat' – consists solely of words spelt out phonetically. A sequence purports to be instructions for making Origami figures ("To make the water, / turn the world over and crease. / Your gnu will fall from the mountain fold / towards sunset.")

This sort of fun is in short supply in contemporary poetry. Now, I'll let you into a secret: I don't really *enjoy* a lot of poetry, period. That's not to say there isn't good stuff out there – poems that are admirably well-crafted, thoughtful, philosophical, intelligent, keenly-observed and a dozen other adjectives. But you can *admire* that without really *enjoying* it, and on the whole you do. There are also plenty of people writing funny, witty, laugh-out-loud, stand-up style verse, which you *enjoy* without really *admiring*. But there's not a lot of intelligent, though-provoking, sensitive, innovative and well-written poetry that also happens to make you smile like you were waking up in the Waking Up Room having just cheated Death and Destruction.

I sometimes think of contemporary British poetry as a Christmas party at the regional tax office. Most of the people there are dressed in appropriate shades – slate grey; sludge brown. They're holding dry white wines and talking in subdued voices about the impact of Basel II. A small group from computing, meanwhile, has donned Hawaiian shirts and comedy bowties. They're laughing far too loudly at each other's 'I'm-mad-me!' antics and photocopying their privates. Gallas would arrive late in a beautifully tailored suit. Made of silk. Bright, sunshine yellow silk. The entrance is unforgettable. Though, if he's not careful, it *will* get him sacked.
Oddly enough, reading Gallas kept reminding me of Reading. Peter Reading, that is. Shurely shome mishtake? I thought so. How could smiley John Gallas have anything in common with a man whose obits described him as "a poet [who]...

took the tradition of British miserabilism to new heights", "like Larkin, only bitter" and "a potty-mouthed Baudelaire", and who himself said "there's no posterity to write for. I'm writing for mutated arthropods"?

Looking closer, though, similarities emerge. They are/were the same generation and both are prolific writers. Both are masters of the themed collection, in which an idea is developed over a number of linked poems. Both are linguistically and formally creative; both are adept at employing traditional forms in novel ways, or to give voice to modern concerns. And both use demotic speech and the odd obscenity to good effect.

Even where they most differ, there are similarities. Reading's cynicism thinly concealed a concern with the world great enough for him to devote 26 books to railing at it; Gallas's smile slips enough to reveal a strain of cynicism. The initial 'Four Thoughts from Abroad', for example, contains a section on the death of a Chinese con man:

Man Ling sold drugs
made out of baking ingredients.

People believed him and died.
He was shot by the sea in Baozhong.

He chose a sailor's suit to die in.
Which shows a kind of care.

Or how about this from 'Death and Fireworks', a poem fundamentally about not wanting to draw the obvious metaphor:

Life is brilliant and short,
with darkness at either end. Get out of *that.*

The fatuous blink of things that mean and know
corrupts my feeling heart.
Piss off please. Don't start.
The Sparrow and the Meadhall. Melting Snow

When you're tired of life, you think notes another poem, which, perhaps, is a good point to introduce 'The Story of Molecule'. 'Molecule' is in fact 'Molloy Gillies', a 12 year old from Gallas's native New Zealand, who leaves home one night on his bike for a series of picaresque adventures in the small towns of South Island. These are related in a sequence of 107 sonnets, and include encounters with the police, fishermen, Maoris, gangs of children, injuries and death, as Molecule strives to escape "the Bastard Evolution".

The debt to Samuel Beckett should be clear. Beckett's Molloy is a vagrant who also heads off on his bicycle for a number of picaresque episodes in identical small towns and the anonymous countryside between. Whereas Molloy is pursued by the anally-retentive private detective Jacques Moran, Molecule has to deal with DS Baigent, the laconic police sergeant who seems always to be eating a Twix. However, the two internal monologues that dominate the sequence – as two dominate Beckett's Molloy – are neither Molecule himself (who speaks a sort of pidgin with occasional, imaginative swearing), nor Baigent (who speaks in pared-down, staccato lines), but Molecule's father Jeff, and a third-person narrator, who describes Molecule's adventures.

Gallas's sure touch in handling these different registers is enormously impressive. Jeff, though revealed as something of a philosopher as the series progresses, talks the slightly down-at-heel language of everyday life:

Zlookin bad,'
said Dad. He snorted. 'Jeff he's probly sitting
up at Nana's' – 'Been there' – 'down at some friend's eh?'
'Phoned em all' – 'or up Poutama Street
with bloody Wig and Steff.' The noontide heat
like lard. Dad drooped. Day 3. 'Jeff you OK?'
The house creaked. Aunty Jack resumed her knitting.

'Dad and Aunty Jack talk'

Molecule's exploits, however, are described in language that veers between the rhapsodic and the mock heroic:

Wavelets blibbed the rippled beach. The knobby
driftwood gleamed. Even the gaunt old pines
danced. Behind, the mountains loomed like proud

parents. Seagulls squawked. A single cloud
stood still above. The long and littered lines
of hightides wrote their careless poetry

'same thing, different direction'

He slept by Grassmere Pond. The water, thick
with sludged and crackled saltshine, glitter-skinned,
shone like Heaven's banner dipped in sin.

'Molecule's dream'

Molecule wants to escape from 'Evolution', which occasionally sounds like small-town life; the opposite of freedom. Elsewhere – indeed, in the odd prose passage I mentioned at the start – Gallas explains that Evolution is "that buried, wonderful part of us", the physical, chemical substance of our brains, that creates and grounds our preferences and responses, and so makes possible (capital letters) Life and Art. "Life's experiences are the twinkly bibbles" (typical Gallas word that – things are always bibbling in these poems) "on a biscuit; but it is these chemicals, these gifts of Evolution, or that unknown part of us... that give us our real Life in its most creative, passionate and committed forms."

So Molecule's ramblings are an extended metaphor for the self's search for artistic and personal freedom. A search made possible by the chemical 'gifts of Evolution', yet which, impossibly, seeks to transcend these gifts, in pursuit of an idea of complete freedom, just as Molecule keeps escaping; keeps bumping into the hard facts of the world; keeps being recaptured.

OK, bottom line. I've bibbled manfully for several pages now. What I'm trying to say is that *Fresh Air and the Story of Molecule* is too large, too strange, too dense and complex, and too downright bloody brilliant to fit the confines of a review. It deserves to win any number of prizes, though I don't suppose it will. There's only one thing for it; you'll just have to go and read it for yourselves.

Ross Cogan

Whitehall Jackals

Chris McCabe & Jeremy Reed
Nine Arches Press £9.99

Setting aside Jeremy Reed's rather irritating introduction to *Whitehall Jackals* that does nothing to whet one's appetite for the poems that follow (he calls it a "Coda-Prefix"), this collaboration with Chris McCabe is engaging, entertaining and evocative. The book took only three months to write and there is certainly freshness and spontaneity in many of the poems from both men that crackle with high voltage linguistic energy. While the preface reads like a 'right on' article in *New Musical Express*, the poems are certainly rewarding and really needed no introduction. They speak, and ought have been allowed to, speak for themselves. It was unnecessary, for example for Reed to explain that "The title *Whitehall Jackals* came out of our mutual disgust with Tony Blair's war atrocities in Iraq, together with his oligarchical political regime of czars, spin, deception and pathological lies..." because this is made abundantly clear in poems such as his 'The Right Hon. Jackal Blair' that make plain the poet's anger in vivid imagery. Victims of the Gulf War, "bacon-rashered Iraq amputees" are memorialized with a power that remind one of Tony Harrison in his 'A Cold Coming', a poet Reed would, in his own terms, dismiss because he says that he and McCabe "have little or no respect for academic poets – formal desk practitioners..." Reed makes the mistake of assuming that poets who are not like him or McCabe are necessarily inferior or perhaps that is just the "zingy chutzpah" he attributes to his own critical faculty.

Reed opines: "To me, if a poem doesn't radically alter your sensory experience of the world and recreate it, then it's of no interest." If he means by this that poetry ought to offer, as Frost said "a fresh look and a fresh listen" then he and McCabe have certainly succeeded. The engagement with and evocation of place is striking and impressive in both poets' work. Reed and McCabe write vividly about the present with a keen eye and ear on the sights and sounds of the past, whether that is the mercantile, poetic, musical, architectural or geological facets of London.

The poems are varied in form. Jeremy Reed's prose poem, 'Mods, Hoodlums, Guttersnipes, Punks' that surveys the wide range of London's popular culture. Chris McCabe is sensitive, like Reed, to the poetic as well as the historic past of London. Eliot's The Wasteland is summoned in 'City of London' and 'Peckham Rye (Hymn for Blake)' revisits the latter's 'London', offering his own vision of the city in a poem that is a diary. Cataloguing what he sees in the city, McCabe starts with a litany of grittily depressing vignettes that repeatedly offer "no vision" or insights but modulates into a more optimistic section in a fractal style redolent of the Irish poet, Desmond Egan, after the April 23 entry. This date is, of course, loaded with the freight of English poetic and national significance. Where Blake, the visionary was also a mystic, McCabe trusts physical sensation "the seraphim of endorphins" as sufficient "for which I give thanks", he concludes. Blake called the senses "the five windows of the soul". Chris McCabe and Jeremy Reed certainly capture the spirit of London, recognising in a Blakean way that the preservation of the city's soul is poetically possible. They are to congratulated for the freshness of their evocative and provocative presentations and re-presentations of London, the specificity of their detailed writing being the most significant factor in their having successfully communicated a powerful sense of its complex whole through its multifarious parts.

Michael Woods

A Discoverie of Witches

Blake Morrison

Lancaster and Sheffield: Litfest and Smith/Doorstop, £12.99

In the *Four Quartets*, T. S. Eliot famously writes: 'Time past and time future / What might have been and what has been / Point to one end, which is always present.' For Eliot, 'Words, after speech, reach / Into the silence' after death, so that 'All is always now.' If Eliot is partly reaching towards a mythical kind of poetry which entirely transcends time, he also talks of the 'co-existence' of past, present and future – which is, of course, not quite the same thing. It is in this latter sense that much of Blake Morrison's poetry – which superficially seems so far removed from Eliot's high-flown rhetoric – aspires to his predecessor's vision, whereby 'All is always now.' In Morrison's remarkable new book, *A Discoverie of Witches*, history is by no means transcended; but rather past, present and future co-exist, interact, clash, overlay one another, to the point that some of his poems become temporal palimpsests.

The 'Preface' to *A Discoverie of Witches* makes clear that this intermingling of past, present and future is ingrained in the very landscape from which Morrison, and most of the poems here originate ('The darkest corner of the realm,' as he describes it elsewhere). Even though the main opening sequence in the book is ostensibly about a 'distant' historical event – the Pendle witch trials of 1612, which resulted in ten people being hung – Morrison writes:

When I was growing up on the Lancashire-Yorkshire border, with Pendle Hill visible in the distance, talk of witches was commonplace; every local village seemed to have one – or rather, every village had an old woman whose behaviour and appearance struck fear into the hearts of children. What happened in 1612 seemed close in time ... [in] the Pennine landscapes I lived among as a child. Bleak moors, rain and wind sweeping over heather, godforsaken spots it feels scary to be in after dusk – this is the territory of witches.

If the apparent 'closeness' of the 1612 witch trials is partly a matter of local geography, it is also a matter of politics – both gender politics, in that the suspicion of old women in these villages is shared across the centuries, and, more generally, the politics of otherness: 'Four hundred years on,' writes Morrison, 'we like to think we handle things better. But ... suspicion and hostility towards the Other persist to this day: it's only the names of the scapegoats that have changed.'

In both poetry and prose, Morrison's work is often a profound expression of empathy for scapegoats, who become all-too-easy foci for a society's deeper problems – from *As If*, his book on the Bulger murderers, to the well-known 'Ballad of the Yorkshire Ripper' (which is included in this volume), to some of the shorter poems here, particularly in the Pendle witches sequence. In 'Old Witches,' for example, the scapegoats are elderly women in general:

The more blind, deaf, lame, arthritic,
hairy-chinned, bowbacked and incontinent,
the greater the power they have.

Their bony hands encircle your wrist,
Their lips issue instructions,
Light the oven, let the cat in, sweep the floor,

Fetch that box of potions from my dresser,
and you do, how can you not,
till the day your patience runs out.

Once they were hanged or drowned.
Today it's more subtle:
a pillow when no one's looking

or an overdose of morphine

– a kindness to them as well as to you.

On first glance, the first three stanzas appear to be based firmly in the past – particularly given their context, as part of a sequence about the Pendle witches – whilst the last two stanzas draw a comparison between past and present, 'once' and 'today.' But actually, 'once' and 'today' disconcertingly co-exist in the poem, and the language quantum-wavers between them, making the reader see double: the poem, that is, plays tricks with time to make its political point, and the 'Old Witches' of the first three stanzas are simultaneously both those of the past *and* the present. Our perceptions and treatment of these scapegoats is trans-historical, and only the mode by which society rids itself of them has changed – from being 'hanged or drowned,' to 'a pillow' or 'an overdose of morphine.'

If the trans-historical structure of poems like 'Old Witches' disconcerts the reader for political reasons, elsewhere this mingling of past and present is intensely poignant – no more so than in 'Gisburne Park,' where the modern hospital is haunted by its rather more joyful past:

The thin-ribbed pillars in the entrance-hall
are the ones you came through for the Hunt Ball.

Beyond Reception and the waiting wheelchairs
was where you drank champagne by marble sculptures...

... after port and coffee, you'd pass out
into the floodlit garden, to waltz and foxtrot

where a band played in the sagging, striped marquee.
Today there's just a lawn, six hoops in it for croquet,

rusting now, as if the spirit had slipped through
them of the place and era – and of you.

But the floor upstairs, where you queued in Fifties dresses
for the Ladies, is crowded still, with nurses

at their stations to direct me to the room
where you lie, worn and nametagged, like a pilgrim

at journey's end. I hold your hand as I held it

then, seeing you dressed and powdered to go out,

a child, beside myself, unable to stop, again
and again pleading for you to stay – and again,

now, despite myself, by your bed, pleading the same.

In this poem, the past and the present are brought into a painful proximity, often within the same two-line stanzas; as Eliot would have guessed, the present is disturbingly haunted by time past, the 'journey's end' by its beginnings. Like so much of Morrison's powerful poetry, what 'Gisburne Park' brings to consciousness is the pain, grief, horror, and even violence inherent in the *un*-peaceful co-existence of past, present and future – in, that is, Eliot's ultimately terrifying idea that 'All is always now.'

Jonathan Taylor

New and Collected Poems
Ruth Fainlight
Bloodaxe Books, £20

2010, the year of Ruth Fainlight's 80th birthday, also marked the timely publication by Bloodaxe Books of her collected poems and translations. *New and Collected Poems* encompasses a remarkable body of work, written over a period of 50 years, including a new collection dating from 2010. The book includes Fainlight's acclaimed collection of poems, *Sugar-Paper Blue,* originally published in 1997 and shortlisted for the Whitbread Poetry Award. *New and Collected Poems* also features work from Fainlight's chapbooks, a reminder that the chapbook format is the life blood for many poets.

In terms of organisation, 'collected poems' type publications often follow a chronological course in presenting the artist's work. Ruth Fainlight's *New and Collected Poems* offers a variation on this theme, as it navigates her oeuvre, thereby surprising the reader and challenging their expectations. Back-to-front, *New and Collected Poems* opens with Fainlight's most recent work, then taking the reader back in time to Fainlight's first collection, *Cages*, published in 1966, and progresses through her work, incorporating her chapbook publications and translations. Each book/chapter reads as a 'stand-alone' piece; however, reading them in succession allows the reader an appreciation of Fainlight's voice. Her poems have a complex energy. They are a celebration of her acute ability to observe life in its detail, the everyday, the shifting dynamics of relationships, and the authenticity of memory.

The opening section of *New and Collected Poems*, entitled 'New Poems', presents Ruth Fainlight's most recent poetry. The first poem in this sequence, the haunting 'The Empty Lot', returns to childhood's past territories. Treating the topics of home and belonging, through exploring the symbolic and physical dimensions of 'space', the poem also has historical significance. 'The Empty Lot' evokes the poetic persona's memories from the wartime years, describing a marginal or liminal space, situated on the outskirts of town, an unpaved street with few neighbours, which the poetic persona inhabits. Referred to as an 'empire', the 'empty lot' is made to represent a liberation or freedom of sorts. Beckoning the reader into this location, the poem reclaims childhood's resilience and authentic, exhilaration and fearlessness: 'To stand waist-high/in the surf of weeds,/bare feet and dusty toes [...] legs scratched by dry stalks/and burrs, bitten by ticks.' The poignant phrase, 'bliss – although/I did not know it yet', with its mid-line pause, foregrounds the passing of time, and encourages the reader to dwell on this moment. 'The Empty Lot' underlines the significance of claiming a space in a world where 'we were strangers', 'isolated'. In contrast, Fainlight's early poem 'The Ante-Room', from her first collection, *Cages* (1966), describes a symbolic inner space, which is solitary and tomb-like. 'This room of stone', in which the poetic persona exists in a state of anticipation; 'I'm only in the ante-room/Of waiting, have learned nothing yet', explores the ideas of place and belonging, by imagining the self in the process of change; 'old selves [...] hang dead as empty coats'.

New and Collected Poems echoes with recurrent preoccupations. Ruth Fainlight returns to the moon motif, and the inspirational figure of the muse, throughout her oeuvre. The poems 'Gloria' and 'The Muse' (both from *To See the Matter Clearly* (1968)) both re-imagine the conventionally gender-coded relationship between the artist and the muse. Several poems treat topics related to religion and spirituality, such as the questioning poems 'God's Language' and 'Lilith' from *The Region's Violence* (1973), musing 'what was God doing', in the poem 'What' from *Burning Wire* (2002). Raging at physical limitation, the poem 'Whatever' from *Sugar-Paper Blue* (1997) explores the mind-body relationship with 'urgent impatience'. The powerful memories evoked by confrontation with past places are evident in the poem 'Hendon Central', again from *Sugar-Paper Blue*. The figure of the sibyl is another recurrent motif in Fainlight's work which continues to resonate and intrigue - in fact, Fainlight's poem 'The Cumaean Sibyl

II', from *Sibyls and Others* (1980), was the TLS poem of the week in late August: 'those withered breasts can still let down/celestial milk to one who craves/ redemption'.

As the poem 'The Cumaean Sibyl II' demonstrates, some of Ruth Fainlight's most significant poems in *New and Collected Poems* treat the topic of ageing. 'A Different Form', from *New* Poems (2010), depicts the physical processes of change and growing older. The poem opens with a series of stark, grotesque parallels between the ageing human body and food going off: 'white spots/on the cheese and green streaks of mould'. Fainlight's use of contrasting colours renders this process at once vivid and abstract; 'sooty black spores on slices of bread', alliteration underlining the flow of the line, the physicality of the image, and the process it depicts. The poem closes on a reminder to see beyond the ageing exterior, returning, in a cyclical movement which emulates the life cycle, to the metaphors rehearsed in the earlier parts of the poem. 'The same immortal energy' flows through both forms.

When comparing 'A Different Form', to one of Ruth Fainlight's early poems on ageing and mortality, called 'Everyone Dies', from *Cages* (1966), the latter poem takes a different direction. 'Everyone Dies' deals with the relationship between the parental generation and its children, evoking the poetic persona's own ambivalent emotions regarding her parents, 'Every time my parents went out I thought they would die./I never looked for their return' and sibling, 'I planned to sell the house. Loaded with cash/I'd banish my brother into an orphanage.' 'Everyone Dies' then switches to the present tense and the poetic persona's perspective towards her own child and, with that, a changed perspective on death and closure: 'And now my son/And my fear when he went to play in the park.' These issues, of common humanity, of the complexity of love, the difficulty of letting go, experiences of mourning, and the passing of time, 'as the hour grew later I fatefully put on mourning/ Sure I would never see him again', are crystallised in the final line's emphasis on the inevitability of mortality.

Showcasing Ruth Fainlight's versatility, *New and Collected Poems* furthermore contains her translations of the well-known Portuguese poet Sophia de Mello Breyner's and the Mexican poet Victor Manuel Mendiola's poetry, which are assured and sensitive, and enlightening for readers with an interest in poetry in translation. Also included in the 'translations' section of *New and Collected Poems* are extracts from three ancient Greek plays by Sophocles, reflecting Fainlight's long-standing interest in myth and the classics. Fainlight's translation work shows her appreciation of linguistic nuances, and an empathetic approach to other poets' sensibilities. *New and Collected Poems* is enlightening and exhilarating in equal measure. One of Britain's finest poets, Ruth Fainlight's brilliance and sense for writing acute, compelling poems show no sign of waning.

Charlotte Beyer

Pretty

Ahren Warner

Bloodaxe, £8.95

Pretty is by turns, entertaining, challenging, witty and intriguing. Anyone who might allow themselves to be intimidated by Warner's learning and range of reference needs to remember that readers should do some work. This is not to say, though, that his poems are not accessible – far from it. It is refreshing to read poems that offer some challenge as well as entertainment.

In a letter of 30 May 1878, Gerard Manley Hopkins wrote to his friend (and later Poet Laureate), Robert Bridges, responding to some of the latter's objections to aspects of his poem, 'The Loss of the Eurydice':

> *Obscurity I do and will try to avoid so far as it is consistent with excellences higher than clearness at a first reading…As for affectation I do not believe I am guilty of it: you should point out instances, but as long as mere novelty and boldness strikes you as affectation your criticism strikes me as— as water of the Lower Isis.*

This response is from a poet far superior to the one taking issue. One can imagine some readers taking exception to what they might view as obscurity in Ahren Warner who, like Eliot, gives the reader credit for being able to intuit rather than necessarily understand every allusion, nuance and semantic suggestion at first reading. Warner's poems may well repay re-readings and for some will shine as examples of poems that have been carefully made.

Opening with a sequence called 'Lutèce te amo', the Latin appellation for Paris is immediately deployed and this immediately signals a concern with cultural and linguistic variety.

Warner also has a playfully Derridean mistrust of the possibility of making stable meaning; he is archly aware of the tautologically suspect ground of challenging its very tautological instability, by being forced to apply linguistic structures and forms that are – inescapably – used to articulate any interrogation of them.

'Nervometer', the sequence that concludes *Pretty* is 'after Artaud', whose work could never be termed pretty — Artaud joined and then departed the Surrealists on the political grounds he emulates. Auden's idea that a poem is "a verbal contraption" is apposite when considering Warner's clear delight in the construction of a poem. The contraption he chooses is a form that approximates to the sonnet, being thirteen lines long. There is an attractive edginess to this sequence that engages with a destabilising Artaudian impulse.

There is a counterpoint between the formal grace of Warner's organising principle of what are more or less sonnets to articulate a deep scepticism about the possibilities of language. There is also a destabilising element in the formal choice of thirteen lines that has congruence with an Artaudian position. The tenth poem in this sequence is just one that will resonate for readers familiar with Artaud's distrust of language (not confined to his poems but also vehemently articulated in The Theatre and its Double):

Those for whom a word has a meaning, a manner
Of being, for whom feelings can be classed, classified,

Discussed by degree, are the worst of all bastards.

Warner, as a supremely confident and competent writer is, after Artaud, lauding intuition over the exegetical energies of the academy; something to which, in his professional life, he also belongs. Just as Artaud's mistrust of language sought in his Theatre of Cruelty to communicate in visceral, physical terms, so the braggadocio swagger about the closing sequence in *Pretty* is not the posturing of the poet who wrote them but a sensitivity to the voice he knew we had to hear.

Ahren Warner's poems may be considered obscure by some readers but it is worth recalling Eliot's insistence that a poem need not be fully understood, that it is a 'dark embryo'. There are excellences in these poems, some that are accessible at first reading but there are more that may be appreciated by those who do not share Robert Bridges' capacity to deal with another poet who was rather a handful at further readings.

What is pretty about this collection? Well, the language is alive and vibrant, the formal achievement fine.

Michael Woods

The Blue Den
Stephanie Norgate
Bloodaxe, £8.95

Stephanie Norgate's debut collection, *Hidden River,* marked her as a poet of great subtlety and craft. It was shortlisted for both the Forward Prize for Best First Collection and the Jerwood Aldeburgh First Collection Prize. Her follow up, *The Blue Den,* is even more remarkable. It is a sharply constructed and observant collection that ebbs along the borders of simple definition.

The Blue Den is concerned with the dichotomy of nature and humanity, and explores it in a way that is both original and constructive, giving a voice to the natural world that intrigues and informs in equal measure. The collection appears in an almost ekphrastic way, with Norgate's talent for rich and evocative imagery seeming to draw parallels between poetry and visual artistry. Images are painted out until the foreground unearths a complete picture that resists the simplicity of her language. Norgate possesses the skill of understatement, a case in point being 'Oriel Window':

Wine Dark Dahlias
in a turquoise vase
in the window
over the bay
correspond
with the one
red light
of the single
fishing boat
returned
for the night.

The red curve is
a Japanese stroke
on the dark blue sea.

what is being said
by colour
That we cannot say?

This poem could easily be written after a piece of artwork, such is the intensity of the vision it provides. The final stanza reads as a challenge, despite being a question that has already been answered by what precedes it. Here Norgate is able to observe the cyclic aspect of nature in a way that is as poignant as it is engaging. These tropes are at their best in 'The Rave Murals at Racton Tower', five frantically paced sestets that layer images into a rounded view of a defaced monument. 'View from the basement' meanwhile traces artistry back to primitive still lives, described as "double selves talking over the world".

There is a channelling of the Shaman in the way these poems are deployed, however they still retain their originality in imagery and suggestion. The writing here is busy with nuanced ideas regarding the way we interact with nature, and it is coloured with nostalgia, affection and sometimes humour. These latter efforts are at odds with the seriousness of the overall collection though, and as such are undermined despite being perfectly good poems in and of themselves.

Norgate impresses in the way she navigates each vignette with a rhythm and tone that flows as evenly and smoothly as the rivers and winds that are present within the nature she describes. *The Blue Den* is imperiously paced, with an attention to rhyme and tempo. The ekphrasis of her poetry is never more evident than in her 'Other Voices' poems, that are laced throughout the collection as grounding presence that redirects the tensions of the poetry into stark and luminous efforts at communication with the outside world. These pieces were a result of Norgate's collaboration with painter Jayne Sandys-Renton, and were originally part of an installation at the Otter Gallery entitled *The Fallen House and Other Voices*. These poems are intensely musical, as they were intended for the spoken word, but also transformative pieces that hint at movement and progress. 'Other Voices: Stream to Ice' is an example of this:

> *I wasn't expecting this change of being,*
> *this suspension of slow, these notes that stones*
> *chip from our shared surface of rime. You don't flinch*
> *at the scatter of flints, or dry sticks hurled*
> *to strike the sound from us.*

Here the personification of a freezing stream communicates the stalling of a natural process, with an emphasis on fricatives giving way to the harsher, more plosive sounds. Norgate knows very intimately what she is trying to communicate, and does so with a constancy that makes *The Blue Den* an altogether more compelling and cohesive a collection than *Hidden River*.

Her penchant for unmeasured couplets is a device that crops up time and again, allowing her to control the pace of observation. There is a kinetic energy in much of these poems that enhances the obsession with nature and its processes. 'Storm and the tea cup' attests this, with its couplets insisting that "You cannot tame the cliffs easily / into a background of white chalk / You cannot hold the sea lens / of a wooden casement / or swivel a tornado / in the cup left on the sill." Here Norgate observes how nature's elements are a constant exercise in resistance. And it is here that the collection uncovers a tension between nature and mankind.

The Blue Den is a place of transgression, frustrated identity and transformation. Man-made objects such as "The Table" in the poem of the same name constantly fail to reconcile with their natural counterparts of trees and fauna. While nature is described vividly and sensuously, it is ultimately frustrated in its attempts to infiltrate the dominance and destruction of humanity. In 'Other Voices: Ant to Sky' the former is adamant in their assertion that they are a "creature that you cannot tame." Knives, windows and flowers (in particular daffodils) appear as totems, symbols of destruction, separation and growth. Norgate seems to see her pale reflection in all that she observes, but fails to imprint, struggling against forces of separation. These are the themes that make *The Blue Den* such an intriguing place. It is a place of beauty but also of decay. Its terrain is navigated with a fluidity and rapidity that can only yield admiration for the poet. Lurking beneath the exterior flourishes of these poems are difficult questions about how we can construct our identities amidst a maelstrom of seemingly contradictory forces.

These poems hover close to the senses and then dissipate into the realms of memory and contemplation. They are explosive packages that trade images for ideas, but they are also more than this. In the words of Robert Frost, these poems begin in delight and end in wisdom. *The Blue Den* is much more than an exercise in poetic competencies and composition, they are vignettes translated into raw units of meaning regarding the state of the world we live in. Ordinarily these high concepts would not work, but Norgate navigates them with such simplicity and lack of condescension that they are brilliantly resonant amongst the current climate of British poetry. She has a gift for subtlety of expression, and also for clarity. *The Blue Den* is thoroughly impressive, a genuinely thought-provoking collection from an accomplished poet.

Ashleigh Davies

Waiting for Bluebeard

Helen Ivory

Bloodaxe, £9.95

My favourite public toilet – please bear with me here – is in Salisbury. For those who know Salisbury, it's the one near the multi-story shoppers' car park. For those who don't, I'll explain that what makes it special is the mirrored wall. As you walk in, you have to pass a floor-length reflective surface. However, these are no ordinary mirrors; they slightly but noticeably distort your image like a milder version of the hall or mirrors from an old fashioned funfair. I think this is wonderful. In fact, I can stand in front of them swaying gently backwards and forwards until either I remember what I've come in for, or else the other occupants begin to stare at me.

Of course, it could be that the mirrors – in truth more of a 'metallic reflective surface' – were incompetently fitted. But I like to think that, somewhere in the bowels of Salisbury City Council's public amenities department resides a council officer who believes that people need to be reminded just how shifting and unreliable are the foundations upon which we build our lives, how untrustworthy our perceptions. Oh inspired situationist amongst council officers, I salute you!

I thought of the Salisbury public toilets several times while reading *Waiting for Bluebeard*. A poem called 'Hosanna', with its mirror-backed mixture of the mundane and the surreal, particularly called them to mind:

The pawnbroker's window
is crowded with mirrors,
with freshwater pearls
and a clock-face pushed to the glass.

In truth, though, the whole collection has that distorting, disorientating feel to it, which can make the ordinary appear monstrous and leave you swaying back and forth trying to restore your focus. If you'd rather not think of toilets, think instead of another strange little room – completely unremarkable on the outside, but extraordinary on the inside – the backroom at the fancy-dress outfitters where Mr Benn enters, only to emerge again through a magic door into a world of strange adventures. Like the odd, fez-wearing proprietor, these poems want to tempt you through the door and show you new landscapes – landscapes like ours but ever so slightly disturbed. Welcome to Ivoryworld.

I personally have always located Ivoryworld somewhere in central Europe, perhaps somewhere in the former Austro-Hungarian Empire that later spent decades under communist rule without quite losing its identity: Bohemia, perhaps, or – why not? – Transylvania. And I see in Helen Ivory points of comparison with poets like the Estonian Doris Kareva or the Slovenian Tomaz Šalamun. All three have the ability to craft beautifully clear, striking images, images which at first can seem unlikely, but which nonetheless work their way into your head until they change the way you perceive the world. So, for example, when Ivory tells you that:

> *There is a kind of singing that turns winter on its hinge,*
> *that wakes animals from their long sleep*
> *and places birds on the highest shelf of the sky*
>
> 'My Mother's Room'

or

> *The thought rises up*
> *like a singing clock,*
> *its bird constructed*
> *of feathers and springs*
>
> 'The House of Thorns'

you know that, with time, that's how you'll see them yourself. Of course winter swings on its hinges, and the sky is a system of shelves where you might store the odd bird. And if your thoughts about this are changing, perhaps it's because they've gained some feathers, or the spring's unwound.

At a time when few British poets look far beyond Britain for inspiration – and those that do look mainly to the US – Ivory's connection to European modernism is one of the things that makes her work rare and exciting. If we're playing the game of influences here, we might explain some of this in terms of the influence of George Szirtes, who taught her at the Norwich School of Art, and who provided flap copy for earlier collections. Of course, this game is of dubious merit. Szirtes himself, for example, claims to look at least as much to America as to Central Europe. So, perhaps Ivory would reject this characterisation of herself. Nevertheless – for me at least – Ivoryworld is a place of thick pine forests, where snow carpets the ground for four months of the year and the mountaintops all year round; where the unwary can suddenly disappear; and where "when the dark clears its throat / dogs and wolves look down from the sky / and the four winds race from their caves."

If in one sense Ivory is a remarkably international poet, there's another – just as remarkable – in which she is very English. *Waiting for Bluebeard* is described as a quest to understand how a girl could grow up to be the woman living in Bluebeard's castle. Bluebeard, of course, is a French folktale of a violent aristocrat who repeatedly murders his wives and hangs their bodies on hooks in his cellar. Despite being feared in the locality, he persuades the daughter of one of his neighbours to become his next wife and the scene is set for what sounds like the plot of a psychological thriller.

The book falls into two parts. Part II takes place in Bluebeard's house, and includes the wonderful sequence of poems entitled 'The Disappearing'. From the first, where "The tariff for crossing the threshold / was a single layer of skin" and:

She didn't imagine the scarring
nor the painstaking care required

to leave the ghost of herself
on the doorstep like a cold-caller

to the last, where "she saw the room's plunder / floating in the dark liquid / of neatly labelled jars", they are so rich and strange that it's hard to separate the strands of fear and love. Are we witnessing someone dying by degrees, or losing their individuality in a passionate relationship? In the folktale, the bride is saved by her brothers and all ends happily. But here she sees her own "skin hung from a wire hanger / on the back of a door / like a wedding dress", and the collection ends with an even more disconcerting – and nursery rhyme-like – poem called 'Hide', in which the nameless narrator dresses in the skin of a dog and walks into the fire. We're left wondering whether she in fact desires her own disappearance; whether Bluebeard's attraction is not in fact his wealth, but the mixture of sadness and menace he exudes as he "sobs like a wolf / from his leather armchair."

What could have brought someone to that? According to the cover blurb "the story begins with a part-remembered, part-imagined childhood." To me, though, elements of it sound very much like a 1970s childhood. The very first poem describes the woman's pregnant mother watching the 1969 moon landings. Others describe a tour coming to Luton ('Jonah the Giant Whale') or what sound like 70s beach holidays ('Trampoline', 'My Father and the Sand Boat'). Yet others reference events like the royal wedding ('Quarantine' – and we all know which royal wedding it has to be.) Given that she was born in Luton in 1969, it's legitimate to ask whether the bride in Bluebeard's castle is Helen Ivory herself.

Of course she's playing with us (I've met her husband; he's charming and beardless). But in the process she's also playing with the conventions of contemporary British poetry, much of which is stuck in a mode that I'd describe as 'domestic/nostalgic'. In other words, its inspiration is drawn from the writer's home life or past, and deals with family members, relationships, memories and so on. Now, to give some perspective to what follows, I should own up to the depth of animosity that I harbour towards poetry of this sort. In fact, if I ever have to hear another poem about someone's grandparents, I swear I'm going to disembowel the author with the potato fork that granddad so lovingly cleaned and oiled and stored in his grass-smelling shed, and then dispose of the body by boiling it down in granny's spotless brass cooking pots. This sort of stuff is just about bearable in the hands of a Seamus Heaney, but the rest of us should observe a moratorium.

Anyway, it's a measure of Ivory's skill that she got not just granny, but a whole gaggle of family members past me without triggering the kill response. She weaves fairytales and dark myths through the poems ("My mother's babies / were undoable knots / stolen from her womb / but the fairies, she said" – 'The Stolen Babies') so that the mixture of the everyday with surreal and startling images both entrances and surprises, and the ground is continually moving under your feet. I particularly admired, for example, 'My Grandmother's Lodger' – who turns out to be Death:

She used her hand-cranked machine,
while Death whizzed ahead with electricity.
They sat at the same table, and when she made tea
he took it stewed with three sugars.

He was quicker on straight runs,

But, of course, granny had the advantage when it came to the detailed work. And so does Ivory. I hadn't thought it possible to breathe life into British domestic poetry, but *Waiting for Bluebeard* – perhaps because it is so open to influences from other traditions – shows how it can be done. This collection – her fourth with Bloodaxe – is her best to date and firmly establishes Helen Ivory as one of the country's most interesting poets.

Ross Cogan

Accurate Measurement

Adam White

Doire Press €12

Accurate measurements are clearly what poems ought to be and Adam White measures up in terms of what he is clearly attempting in his work. Whilst he is certainly accurate and sometimes measured, he is also expansive and open. I use the term 'attempting' in its most positive sense; a serious climber makes an attempt at a difficult rock face or summit. In a self-conscious and deliberating way but can never plan entirely for the unexpected Indeed, the business of making, unmaking and remaking is a consistent theme in this collection.

Some of the poems in *Accurate Measurements* take Heaneyesque approaches; the loops and whorls of his poetic fingerprint are discernible but never smudge over the distinctiveness of a poet who works words with a skill that is all his own. While Heaney famously decided to dig with his pen, White takes up the tools of his own earlier trade of carpenter, exploiting the metaphorical possibilities it affords with well-judged craft. Added to this, there is a genuine affection for the trades he describes, and sites he has worked on, in a way that celebrates the dignity of manual work, admiring, in Hopkinsian fashion, all trades and their gear.

The opening poem, 'Roofing' describes a process from the inside. The procedure of roofing and the tools needed for the job are described in a way that deftly captures the simultaneity of rough and ready manual work but also the expertise of tradesmen. Familiarity allows White to give us sharply observed details: "Depending on the weather, deal wall plates / slap or clonk into place." The solid physicality as well as the phonic nuances are finely realized. A tremendous simile in the second stanza describes "...lean rafters, like joined hands, are / raised to reverence to Pythagoras, / who was one of us." The geometrical accuracy of measurement is common to the ancient Greek mathematician and the modern day roofer. The helpful, practical application of theory in a real life situation reminds us that we must not underestimate what manual work involves. There is also a self-reflexive dimension to the poem by the time its conclusion is reached:

Take your time as you alight form the lashed ladder,

hit the ground before the evening's first rain;
tomorrow you will do it all again.

Just as the roofer is involved in a process again and again, so too is the poet engaged in a process of making and shaping that is repeatedly returned to.

Just as Seamus Heaney had, as he said, his "first jolt from Hopkins", and then a sense of "permission" after reading Hughes' *The Hawk in the Rain*, White has clearly felt both the jolt of Heaney's language and permission from the nature of some of his subject matter. White has clearly read Heaney with the sense of gratitude that the late, great Seamus read, for example, Hopkins, Kavanagh and Hughes. Since White so openly acknowledges the example of Heaney, it is well worth citing how the latter provided an accurate measure of what makes an authentic poetic voice. In *Preoccupations, Selected Prose 1968-1978*, the opening chapter 'Feelings into Words', Heaney says:

> *Finding a voice means that you can get your own feeling into your own words and that your words have the feel of you about them; and I believe that it may not even be a metaphor, for a poetic voice is probably very intimately connected with the poet's natural voice, the voice that he hears as the ideal speaker of the lines he is making up.*

White achieves what Heaney describes. Although we can detect the impulse of 'Digging' in 'In June', a poem about the burial of the family dog, the voice is his own:

Above in bed, I heard the shovel —
or perhaps it was a spade —
slicing soil, some of which my mother made
by carrying those bucket full

of juice-losing peel to the barrel in
the garden:
my sister stabbing
with belief down into the guts
of the black garden. The order
given: quarry a last place for
a decomposing dog…

There is mordant wit in "Shall I throw a bone / in with him?" followed by a mother's order to " 'Get it done.' " and a conclusion that signals regret at the creatures passing: "I should have written: / *Dubh — thank you for having been here. The dog's name was* 'black', rather like the atmosphere of the poem and the earth in which it is buried.

Many poems delight in this collection. The tender 'Travelling Back' is made more so as a result of its emotional understatement, while 'Dawn Light' offers another impressive reflection of the place of writing, its physical and psychic sources. The latter is a poem that one reads with deepening admiration for its straightforward concreteness that is nonetheless pregnant with a sense of illumination beyond the obvious light sources mentioned in the poem. The poet cannot simply hole up in poetry as "just a place to hide" but must "unbolt the door and go outside".

The concluding poem of the collection is a moving leaving of one of the Western Islands for the mainland. It presents the past having to come to terms with the realities of the present but also affirms the power of nature – the land that was claimed by humans is reclaimed by the sea. Whilst the poem itself engages with the complexities of human settlement, it does so in direct and unfussy language, and this is in keeping with the solid verities with which White persistently engages. He is a celebrator of the ordinary as that which opens portals to the extraordinary. The fact of being grounded is what allows him the purchase to become airborne.

Michael Woods

A Place Where Animals Stand

Simon Williams

Oversteps Books £8.00

The poems in *Where Odd Animals Stand* are very wide-ranging in their subject matter, style and form. Williams engages with childhood, parenthood, illness, history, science and the preservation of goats, none of that species being harmed in the writing of his book. There is a gentleness of voice pervading the collection: humanity and humour with no hubris. Simon Williams is at home in a wide range of verse forms including villanelle, sonnet and free verse and deploys them to good effect at various points in the collection.

'Petrarchan Sonnet' is funny. It is also clever in its self-referential nature, concentrating on the rhyme scheme itself. Addressing Petrarch, Williams asks:

"Working as a scholar, did you fore c / how all your words would flow for one lay d? Beyond its wit, this poem does not seem contrived because it is clearly poking fun at contrivance as well as obsession. Added to this, Williams is up to the job of making.

Williams' earlier book, *Quirks*, is an unsurprising title given the fact that he certainly has a penchant for the unusual, and it is quirkiness that often characterises his writing. A photographed goat stands in the road on the front cover of the book and, on the back cover is a picture of its behind. The two moments captured by a camera shutter offer a pleasing pictorial equivalent to the whole procedure of Simon Williams' collection that very effectively presents the reader with an image of invitation and departure. It is not a particularly odd animal but it looks odd standing in the road. It looks curious but ready. Williams is clearly seeing his title as a metaphor for the manner in which poems can come unexpectedly but it is the job of the poet to confront the reader with some odd animals. In other words, it is important to remind the reader that the ordinary is a doorway into the extraordinary.

It is difficult to highlight poems from this collection as so many are worthy of comment. 'Sixty Seven', for example, recalls a Father's heart attack. The deliberate ambiguity of the title names 1967 as the year of "the July or August of Love", but also signals the age his father was when he had a heart attack. Instead of concentrating on the detail of trauma, Williams understatedly mentions first that his father was "short of breath" and moves in the following stanza to report that "Mr Yacoub took my dad in hand, / bypassed all his furred connections..."

'Late Blackberries' recalls the poet's own heart attack and rehabilitation, the ordinary experience of picking blackberries with his daughter a renovating one that leads him to recognize the possibility of recalibrating life by finding, as he observes, "new ways to exercise our hearts".

'28 Weeks', dedicated to Matt, presumably, Williams' son is a beautifully tender poem with a light touch but a telling impact. The baby developing in its mother's womb has two months left before birth. The expectant mother is observed by the expectant father. The poem concludes with: "You're getting older, to the point / when you'll be no years old". This poem certainly exercises the heart.

Above all, *A Place Where Odd Animals Stand* is a most enjoyable, life-affirming read and there are plenty of poems in this absorbing collection that are well worth returning to for their sensitivity and expansiveness, that engage most sensitively with what is worth cherishing in life.

Michael Woods

Long Exposure at Cordoba

Katherine Crocker

Indigo Dreams Publishing

Katherine Crocker writes thoughtful and attractive poems, spare in their presentation and form. Rooted in nature, narratives play out against the backdrop of changing seasons, shifting continents and lengthening shadows. Her concerns are wide ranging, from refugees, to childhood memories to complicated lives and love affairs.

She admires Amadou from Segou, a wheelchair bound young man who 'dreams of an office job, a wage' who lives in the 'red street dust.' She is impressed by his resilience and above all his hope. He tells her: 'Today is a great day' and sells poems to make a living - an impressive feat even in this country. They share a love for the sound of language and its transformative power:

Words not translated, sing out,
music in different tongues.

Elsewhere, in 'Mud', a man walks along a riverbank, with an opened letter in his pocket, carrying a secret. The title suggests a misdemeanour, a dilemma, while the river and fields reflect the altered reality: 'the silt tells the story of a changed land.' The man reflects on what he will say to his son about his new situation. Not everything is explained in her poems:

Tomorrow he will tell him, no more secrets,
tell him straight.

The poems are accompanied by evocative, allegorical line drawings, again blessed with a natural lyricism, almost Japanese in its pastoral symbolism, which give the book both pace and space; they are places empty of language where the eye and ear can rest between the written pieces. They come from the same place as the poetry however - humanity's relationship with natural world, constantly in flux.

The poem 'Kale Field' is a clue to the origin of this deep affinity with nature:

Kale so tall we were hidden all afternoon
nestled in willow herb

From the safety of the undergrowth, they see her Dad, presumably a farmer, raises a knife 'three times as he plunged the steel/through swollen flesh, calves gorged on kale.' There is almost a Biblical menace in this description, which contrasts sharply and effectively with the childlike innocence of the 'the hidey hole' and 'the trampled stalks where we made our den.' She writes with genuine clarity and feeling, reflecting emotion and memory on the ever changing palette of fields, crops and flushed red skies.

She is not afraid to experiment with language too. There is interesting repetition used in the poem 'Snake, Choeung, Ek', where phrases appear, disappear then reappear, mimicking the elusive behaviour of the snake itself. It opens as 'Something slithers in the mud' then later: 'something slithers in the grass.' It is a painterly technique, unusual and original - suggesting her interest in visual art is informing the written word.

Occasionally her poems feel like they may have had their origin in a workshop; 'About Time' is Cinderella retold:

It's after midnight when she runs home,
slips through the back door.

It is in poems like these that I found the poetry slips a little into prose where the idea takes over from the language. The opening line for me is not strong enough: 'The clock strikes ten as she walks into the hall.' She is perhaps keen to engage the reader from the outset, but originality of expression is as important as clarity. It is when ideas and language are allowed to unravel together when Crocker's poetry really soars, as in the classically influenced sonnet, 'Daphne'. A woman and tree have somehow become intertwined:

The tree splits, reaches to another sun,
pink arms flesh green.

The description is sensual and visceral as a male protagonist also becomes involved: 'Sap pales her blood/seeps through his hands/wrapped round her waist.' It is suggestive of different lives, different minds, different desires and does not attempt a firm resolution. Again classical and Biblical references are inferred but metamorphosis is the predominant theme. Both the natural world and human emotions are shimmering, elusive - always changing, unless caught for a moment in pen and ink.

Christopher James